Seiyu Kiriyama, Chief Abbot of the Agon Sect of Buddhism

# 21st Century: The Age of *Sophia*

# 21ˢᵗ Century: The Age of *Sophia*

The Wisdom of Greek Philosophy and
the Wisdom of the Buddha

by

## Seiyu Kiriyama

The Chief Abbot of
the Agon Sect of Buddhism

Translated by Rande Brown

HIRAKAWA SHUPPAN INC.

Copyright © 2000 by Seiyu Kiriyama
All rights reserved. No part of this publication may be reproduced
without prior permission in writing from the publisher.

First published in 2000 by
HIRAKAWA SHUPPAN INC.
Mita 3-1-5, Minato-ku, Tokyo 108-0073, Japan

Japanese-English Translation by Rande Brown
In collaboration with
Michiko Abe and Fukiko Kai
Designed by Akihiko Tanimura
Printed and bound in Japan by
NISSHA Printing Co., Ltd.
Paper Supplied by Nakasho, Inc.

Translated from the Japanese original,
first published in 2000 by HIRAKAWA SHUPPAN INC.,
under the title *21 Seiki wa Chie no Jidai.*

# Contents

Part II

# Agon Buddhism:
# The Religion of Wisdom

Addendum
The record of a lecture delivered at
The National Buddhist Seminary
of China (Buddhist College)

# About Agon-shu

# Prologue

# From the 'Century of Fear' to the 'Century of Wisdom'

The 20th century has been a century of fear. It has been the age of anxiety symbolically prophesized by Nostradamus in his writings.

The science and technology that were supposed to bring the human race comfort and convenience have produced a steady stream of deadly, destructive weapons.

Humankind has created a host of problems, any one of which could spell the end of our future : nuclear warheads, destruction of the environment, or pollution of our food sources could all bring disaster, to say nothing of the ongoing danger we face from war and civil upheaval.

Reflecting on our plight always reminds me of Arthur Koestler, the author of *The Ghost in the Machine* who was so despondent over the nuclear capacity of modern civilization that he committed suicide. His depression was fueled by his belief that there is a flaw in the design of the human brain that has forced us inexorably into these desperate straits.

(For more on this topic, please refer to my book *Kanno Shiko* [Interbrain Thinking].)

There is an ancient Indian myth, a prophecy really, that foretells the coming of 1000 wise men to save the earth from a catastrophe.

This ancient myth was incorporated into the corpus of Buddhist thought, where it emerged in a variety of different forms. We find it, for example, in the sutra *Names of the Thousand Buddhas of the Present Age of Wisdom*. We see an ultimate version of it in the diamond realm mandala, a central iconographic representation of wisdom in esoteric Buddhism. This mandala has at its center a fundamental grouping of deities known as the attainment body assembly. Surrounding them, filling the space inside the second border of the submandala, is a company of deities known as the thousand buddhas of the present age.

These are the thousand buddhas of the age of wisdom.

And this is why esoteric Buddhism refers to this time on earth as the age of wisdom.

I suggest that the word 'age' here may be interpreted to mean 'century'. Hence, we might suppose that this is the century in which the wise men will appear to save the world from destruction.

Doesn't it sound plausible that the someday of this ancient prophecy is the today of the here and now?

*As she stands facing the advent of the 21st century,*
*'Spaceship earth' keens in distress under the threat of chaos*
*and destruction.*

*She is wandering about without firm direction, desperately*
*seeking a way out of her predicament.*

*The only thing that can save her from destruction is*
*unsurpassed wisdom.*

There are two forms of wisdom that represent the highest achievements of the human race.

One is the wisdom of philosophy that arose in the West.

The other is the wisdom of Gotama Buddha that originated in India.

I am profoundly interested in comparing these two types of wisdom. This motivation is grounded in more than simple curiosity. I believe that our present situation makes such comparison a matter of vital importance.

And this is because these two forms of wisdom have been crucial in the creation of their respective civilizations.

On the one hand we have

Western (Judeo-Christian) ... scientific ... materialistic civilization.

And on the other,

Eastern (Indic-Buddhist) ... spiritual ... non-materialistic civilization.

Western civilization has been leading the world for the last 2000 years. It has generated a great deal of success, but now looks like it is approaching a dead end. If things continue on as they are, the whole edifice of civilization may just collapse.

I suggest that this might be a good time to embrace the wisdom that Eastern civilization has to offer.

I do believe that the human race has a future.

There is one more ancient Indian legend. It follows the one about the wise men of the present age.

This myth, or prophecy, also appears in a sutra, the *Names of the 1000 Buddhas of the Future Age of Constellations*. This scripture predicts a future era on the earth known as the 'age of constellations'. One thousand wise men will arise among the stars in the sky and bring peace and prosperity to a newly reconfigured civilization.

The human race is going to make a great leap forward

from the age of wisdom into the age of constellations!

But we can't forget what comes first. This latter prophecy is predicated on the earlier one. We must first produce the 1000 wise men of the present age. And these are the people who will carry with them the wisdom to overcome the crises we are facing and help us to create a new universal era.

It might behoove us to embrace the glorious wisdom that these buddhas bring.

Part I

# Philosophy:
# The Study of Wisdom

# The Form of Religion and the Branch of Knowledge that Have Pursued Wisdom

In the West, one branch of learning has devoted itself exclusively to the pursuit of wisdom:

Philosophy

In the East, one form of religion has devoted itself exclusively to the pursuit of wisdom:

Agama (Agon, Jp.) Buddhism

An overview of world history presents only two disciplines where wisdom has been pursued solely for its own sake. In the realm of academic scholarship, there is philosophy and, in the world of religion, there is Agon Buddhism. There would appear to be no others.

Buddhism can be divided into three distinct lineages, namely:

Agama (Agon, Jp.) Buddhism

Abhidharma Buddhism

Mahayana Buddhism

Agama (Agon) Buddhism fosters the teachings and methods for acquiring true wisdom that Gotama Buddha taught in the Agama (Agon) Sutras.

Abhidharma Buddhism relies on scholarly texts that were derived from these original sources. It centers on the study of treatises that serve to regulate, comment upon, analyze, and summarize the doctrine that Gotama Buddha taught in the Agama Sutras. The Sanskrit word Abhidharma was variously translated into Chinese as 'great law', 'incomparable law', or 'counter-law'. The honorary appellation 'the true wisdom' implies that the Abhidharma texts have the capacity to generate wisdom.

This name might seem appropriate because of their roots in the Agama Sutras, which do teach the way to wisdom. But I take exception to the use of the term because the wisdom that can be gained from the methods taught in the Abhidharma texts is inherently different from the 'true wisdom' produced by following the methods that were taught by the Buddha.

Abhidharma Buddhism does not give rise to the same kind of pure wisdom that the direct method of the Buddha does. It is a derivative system that was meant to deepen one's wisdom through the reading, studying, and researching of primary sources. This is why I believe that Abhidharma Buddhism should be called a system of knowledge rather than a system of wisdom.

The third lineage, Mahayana Buddhism, focuses on the development of compassion, and all of its sutras are concerned with this subject. There are Mahayana sutras that also deal with the topic of wisdom, but most of these have been taken from Abhidharma sources.

# The Word *Philosophia*

The Greek word for philosophy is *philosophia*. *Philo*

($\phi\iota\lambda o$) means love. *Sophia* ($\sigma o\phi\iota\alpha$) means wisdom. Thus, *philosophia* means 'to love wisdom' or 'the love of wisdom'.

Amane Nishi translated the term into a Japanese word meaning 'the study of clarity' in the late 1800's.

# The Times of
# the Sixth Century B.C.

The sixth century B.C. was an inordinately interesting period. It witnessed the beginning of humanity's quest for wisdom, a search that was begun in both the East and West at practically the same moment.

In the East we see Gotama Buddha begin his search for true wisdom by undertaking a regimen of strict religious austerities. In the West, around the same time, we see a number of men appear in the Mediterranean area who are also looking for the truth. These men live in Greece, a small peninsula jutting out into the sea, and in the Greek colonies of Ionia on the Turkish coast of Asia Minor and in Southern Italy. They are known as 'lovers of wisdom'. They gather together into groups and give birth to what we now know as Greek philosophy.

In passing, we should note that in China, also at this time, Confucius was expounding the ideas that have come down to us as Confucianism.

So, what kind of wisdom were these seekers looking for, and how were they going about their search?

# The Founders of Philosophy, Thales and Heraclitus

At first, the wisdom connoted by the ancient Greek word *philosophein* (to love wisdom) meant objective knowledge about human life and the world.

The first written appearance of the word is found in Herodotus' *History* (I, 30) in a passage about the Athenian wise man Solon (late 7th–early 6th century B.C.). King Croesus of Lydia is quoted as saying to Solon: "Your love of wisdom has fueled your pilgrimage to many different lands." We later find the word in Thucydides' (*c.* 460– *c.* 400 B.C.) *The Peloponnesian Wars* (2, 40). There is an account of Pericles' memorial address to the first fallen soldiers of that war in which he says: "We must not fall into dissipation for the love of beauty nor lose ourselves in effeminacy for the love of wisdom (*philosophoumen*)."

But the *philosophein* and *philosophoumen* of Solon and Pericles do not go beyond a secular kind of knowledge. The wisdom that Solon is searching for, for instance, is one that will help explain secular reality and man's place within it, as he already understands them. It will serve to glorify the gods and rationalize human limitations.

Aristotle (384–322 B.C.) tells us in the *Metaphysics* that Thales (*c.*624–*c.*546 B.C.) was the founder of philosophy (*archegos philosophias*) and this has been the accepted opinion ever since.

The reason that Aristotle says Thales was the founder of philosophy is because he believed that philosophy originated with Thales, that he is the one who opened up

17

the field.

Philosophy first began when someone asked the question: "What is the foundation (the *arche*) of this world?" Philosophy then attempted to explain how the world arose and how it was established in the clear words of truth rather than mythology.

Three early thinkers appeared who asked and tried to provide philosophical answers to this question. The first of these was Thales. He was followed by his two disciples, Anaximander and Anaximenes. All three men were citizens of the Greek colony of Miletus located in the coastal region of Asia Minor known as Ionia. Asia Minor is the body of land that connects Greece and the Orient.

Collectively, these three formed what is known as the Milesian school or the Ionian school of natural philosophy.

Thales based his doctrine on the fundamental proposition that the primary element (*arche*) of the natural world is water.

Thales asserted that "all things are made of water." He began with the supposition that there is something that underlies the phenomenological diversity of the universe, and went on to determine that this thing is water. Nature assumes a multitude of forms, but all of these are a transformed state of the one primal element. Simply, Thales perceived the world as water.

Thales' disciple Anaximander continued with the idea that there is one basic element that makes up the world, but he said that this element is 'boundless' (*apeiron*) and 'infinite'. Anaximander's disciple Anaximenes also followed this basic assertion, but he concluded that the *arche* is air.

And this is how the history of philosophy began.

However, if we agree with the Hegelians that the essence of philosophy is dialectical thought, we might have to conclude that philosophy properly began with Heraclitus (*c.* 500 B.C.), who taught that the world is not fixed but is in constant motion. Or, looking at it from the standpoint of philosophical materialism, we could claim that the field actually began with the atomism of Democritus (*c.* 460–*c.* 370 B.C.). How we define philosophy naturally influences when we think it began.

Aristotle chose Thales as the founder of philosophy because Aristotle believed philosophy begins with a profound sense of wonder (*thaumazein*) that stimulates us to try to understand the source of our awe. Philosophy's purpose is to find a systematic theory that satisfies this urge to know.

I am very interested in Heraclitus' idea that "all things are in a state of flux" because it seems to me that this idea comes from the same base as Gotama Buddha's assertion that "all conditioned things are impermanent," even though the two draw different conclusions from the concept.

Heraclitus came from noble parentage but relinquished his birthright in order to become a life-long scholar and critic. It is said that he never learned anything from anyone else, that all he knew he discovered on his own. He was an aloof and solitary thinker, who accepted no disciples and formed no school.

As we can see from the statement "all things are in a constant state of flux," Heraclitus' idea was that the true nature of the universe is change.

Heraclitus says that the way of the world is the appearance of change. Plato helps to clarify this in his explanation of Heraclitus' philosophy, in which he writes: "Nothing exists. All is becoming." "All things pass and nothing abides." "All things are in motion."

Heraclitus himself says: "All things are ceaselessly moving, identity is in no way continuous. It is becoming, passing away, increasing, or decreasing. There is no instant of stillness as life becomes death and death becomes life."

This sounds like the Buddhist theory of 'The Middle Path of the Eightfold Negation'.[1]

Heraclitus compares existence to a river. He uses enigmatic phrases to explain the facts of nature. "You cannot step twice into the same river for fresh waters are ever flowing in upon you. We step into the same river but we don't step into it. We exist but we don't exist."

Heraclitus means that it may appear like we are stepping into the same river but actually we are not because the river itself is changing instant by instant. It is a mistake to think that flow has an independent identity. The perception of permanence arises because as water flows past a comparable amount of water flows in to replace it. Heraclitus argues that this kind of ceaseless transformation is the universal form. By so doing, he concludes that the beingness of a river (existence) is the same thing as the non-beingness of a river (non-existence). Thus, the universal principle is that change is the only

---

[1]'The Middle Path of the Eightfold Negation.' Nagarjuna's *Mulamadhyama-kakarika* (The Fundamental Wisdom of the Middle Way) begins with these verses explaining the theory of dependent origination : non-birth and non-extinction, non-cessation and non-permanence, non-uniformity and non-diversity, non-coming and non-going.

thing that never changes.

This idea places Heraclitus within the lineage of Ionian natural philosophy.

Hegel places great value on Heraclitus' theories in his *Lectures on the Philosophy of History*, and Nietzsche shows their influence in his notions of the '*Übermensch*' and 'eternal recurrence'.


# Parmenides: Things that Change Are Non-Existent

A philosopher appeared whose ideas were in direct opposition to Heraclitus' theory of 'universal flux.'

His name was Parmenides of Elea (544–501 B.C.).

Parmenides claimed that nothing which changes can actually exist.

Parmenides totally rejects the idea, which sensory experience may lead us to believe, that something can both 'exist and not exist'. Parmenides says that reason (*logos*), mind (*nous*), and thought (*noein*) are the yardsticks by which we must judge reality.

> "Being already is, it cannot come into being nor cease to be. This is because being is not deficient ; it is complete and bounded, and cannot be changed or moved, but remaining the same in the same and on its own lies, and so remains steadily there. Nor was it ever, nor will it be, since

it all is now together, one, coherent. Where can you find any beginning? From where does being arise? I will not allow you to say that being arises from nothing."

(From *Shoki Girisha Tetsugakusha Danpenshu* [A Collection of Fragments of Early Greek Philosophers])

Let us try to explain what he means.

According to Parmenides, the philosophers who preceded him were not able to arrive at the precise distinction between being and non-being. They supported the contradiction that empty space is being. He resolves this contradiction by recognizing the existence of non-being and says that it is nothing, just empty space. Accordingly, because being is not something that can arise out of non-being, it is a unified state that is necessarily unchangeable and immovable, uncreated and indestructible. If this were not true, there would have to be something else (something that doesn't exist) existing somewhere besides this unified existence either at the beginning, in the middle, or at the end of it. In rejecting diversity and mutability, Parmenides is rejecting the way our ordinary sense-perceptions convince us of the illusion that "things that don't exist do" (phenomena arise and pass away, change, move). Using rational thought he finds, instead, that the only thing that truly exists is this perfect worldly sphere, which is unmoving and unchanging, non-becoming and non-ceasing.

Until this point, when philosophers said that something existed they meant that it existed precisely because it moved and changed. But Parmenides was the first to conceive of true existence as something that does not become something else and thus to arrive at a precise distinction between what is true being and what is not.

This distinction would later coalesce into that between true existence (the essentiality of things) and changeable existence (phenomenological existence). But, for now, Parmenides' idea nipped in the bud the dialectical argument that the natural world holds contradictions within itself, that it can move and develop by itself.

Parmenides left two issues for the philosophers that came after him.

The first is that they were not able to dismiss the fact that things are diverse and mutable as sensory illusion. So, even if a philosopher accepts Parmenides theory of being, he or she still has to account for the phenomenological world.

Secondly, Parmenides' idea of being (it is) raises the idea of a perfect, unchanging existence. From this time on, the history of philosophy develops around the axis of the concept of a perfect existence, or ideal. Philosophy began asking the question: "Why is it, why do human beings have the conception of a perfect existence?" This, in fact, strikes at the heart of why philosophy is philosophy, and is something that we will consider later on.

# The Philosophy of Ancient Greece

The present volume, as you can see, is not intended to be a systematic compilation of the history of philosophy or an outline of the subject.

Rather, it is merely an attempt to touch upon and highlight the source points of the branch of knowledge that cherishes wisdom.

My intention was to take a random look at the philosophers who were devoted to finding objective philosophical wisdom and to compare what they found to the wisdom sought by the Buddha.

But any venture of this nature inevitably leads to a discussion of the philosophy of ancient Greece.

According to the *Seiyo Tetsugakushi* (History of Western Philosophy) (Katsutoshi Uchiyama and Sumio Nakagawa, Eds.):

> Above all else, beyond its most profound achievements, ancient Greek philosophy has maintained a constant significance throughout the ages because it has provided us with a clear guide as to what philosophy is and what kind of motivation is needed to sustain it. Since olden times branches of knowledge have taken their names from the language of ancient Greece, but philosophy is the one in particular in which the connection goes much deeper than the name. Diogenes Laertius suggests this when he tells us that "philos-

ophy has resisted being called anything other than its Greek name."

Philosophy comes from the Greek word *philosophia* (to love and seek wisdom). The word and the idea were an original invention of the ancient Greeks to describe the intellectual activity sprouting among them. The movement was driven by the pure desire for mental self-improvement (character development) unrestricted by the necessities of life or mere intellectual curiosity. Philosophy was formulated to systematize all the newly occurring intellectual activity. In a sense, the Greeks may have been the only people who could understand what the 'love of wisdom' meant (as if the implication of the word *philosophia* could only be realized by them). For it is evident, in fact, that the classical age saw the greatest flourishing of philosophical activity and that later philosophical revivals were only possible by returning to these original ideas. Philosophy can never separate itself from *philosophia*.

This certainly seems to be true.

I can't help thinking that such pure love of wisdom, this *philosophia*, may have in fact died with the ancient Greeks.

For the medieval period is not an age of philosophy, but an age of theology.

When we look at the history of Christianity, we see how it grew out of the regional religion of Judaism and turned itself into a major world religion by fully incorporating the achievements of Greek philosophy into itself.

Medieval philosophy was the philosophy of the monastery.

And because the monastery existed for the pure cultivation of the spirit, the philosophy of the monastery naturally turned its focus on God. The efforts that Plato and Aristotle exerted to find the absolute in their search for wisdom was translated by the monastics into the endeavor to prove the existence of the Christian God. Plato and Aristotle are depicted in certain medieval religious paintings as saints wearing haloes.

Beginning with St. Paul and continuing through St. Augustine (354–430), Christian thinkers endeavored to turn Christianity into a universal religion by adopting a theoretical system that was equivalent to that of philosophy.

One issue that deserves later discussion is how this process compares to that which occurred in Buddhism.

Christian theology continued its development with the scholasticism of Thomas Aquinas. Complicated arguments prepared the ground for modern philosophy, which soon emerged onto the world stage in the thinking of Rene Descartes.

# Pythagoras' Metaphysics of Numbers

We now need to go back through time and take up

the subject of Pythagoras (late 6th century B.C.), a philosopher who exerted a deep influence on Parmenides, among many others.

According to one well-known Japanese scholar, Amane Nishi, Pythagoras was the first person to use the word philosophy. Dr. Tozu uses the historical assertion that "Pythagoras insisted on a strict distinction between the words *philosopia* and *philosophos* (love and lover of wisdom) on the one hand, and *sophia* and *sophos* (*sophist*) on the other" to conclude, similarly, that "philosophy, as the love of wisdom, first sprouted forth from Pythagoras and later blossomed in Socrates" (*Tetsugaku Gaisetsu* [Outline of Philosophy]).

And so we can't neglect to mention Pythagoras' name when discussing the founders of philosophy. But even more than that, he is important to our discussion here because of the profound influence that he had on Plato.

The Persians began their conquest of the Ionian colonies of Asia Minor in 546 B.C. Miletus finally fell in 494 B.C., but, by that time, Greek intellectual life had already shifted, in the late sixth century, to various cities in southern Italy (then known as *Magna Graecia*) and Sicily.

Pythagoras was born on Samos, an island off the western coast of Asia Minor, the original cradle of philosophy. We know that he moved to the allied city of Kroton in southeastern Italy in 530 B.C. That is where he founded the school that bore his name and embodied his richly erudite and deeply religio-humanistic characteristics. Pythagoras attracted many disciples who gathered and settled around him.

Heraclitus sings the praises of Pythagoras, saying, "He

possesses a greater amount of intelligence than any other living being," and yet also condemns him as "the original charlatan." It would seem that Pythagoras had a complicated, multi-faceted character.

Pythagoras, like Thales, left no writings behind him, so it is impossible for us to make any clear distinction between his ideas and those of his disciples.

As I noted before, Aristotle chose Thales as the founder of philosophy because Aristotle believed philosophy begins with a profound sense of wonder (*thaumazein*) that stimulates us to try to understand the source of our awe. Philosophy is basically the love of knowledge that impels us to find a systematic theory that satisfies this urge to know. Aristotle believed that Thales and the Milesian school were the first people to have taken this position.

The members of the Milesian school looked at the world and were deeply impressed by its transitory nature, by its perpetual process of birth, growth, decay, and death. This made them want to determine what lay at the foundation of it. As such, they were largely indifferent to religion.

In contrast, Pythagoras and his school were deeply concerned with religious matters. Their way of life was based not only on rational behavior and the pursuit of philosophical wisdom but also on a religious faith that sought the elevation of the soul.

The Milesians and the Pythagoreans were both trying to find the constant unchanging something at the basis of the ever-changing universe. But they looked for it in very different ways.

The Milesians imagined the problem as the search for the fundamental material of nature. They were trying to figure out what the world is made of.

The Pythagoreans were more concerned with identifying the unchanging structure, or form, of the ever-changing world.

The Pythagorean Society believed in the immortality of the soul and in its transmigration. They dedicated themselves to the purification of the soul and developed a celibate lifestyle based on strict, quasi-religious principles.

Essentially, the Pythagoreans believed that the human soul is imprisoned in the flesh of the present body because of sins that it committed in former lifetimes. The soul can only gain release from physical bondage and attain spiritual beatitude through a process of purification.

A soul that is purified is able to extricate itself from its bodily shackles and ascend to the highest heavenly realms. An impure soul is enslaved in the body of the inferior person or animal in which it finds itself and is unable to find any peace.

The Pythagoreans believed that the sullied soul could be virtuously guided towards a state of purified cleanliness.

We see here a significant precursor to the doctrines of Empedocles and Plato, and further note the mystical suggestion that a soul has the potential to turn itself towards the heavenly realm to be unified with God.

Because of their belief in nurturing the soul, the Pythagoreans advocated religious-like rules to promote clean living. They pledged to venerate spirit, honor their parents and elders, respect the law, love country, be loyal to friends, and be temperate in all things. Yet, even though they practiced these tenets in their daily lives, they did not bother to bolster them with any theoretical religious foundation. The Pythagoreans may have preached religious dogma like the transmigration of the soul and retribution in the afterlife, but they did not choose to base their beliefs on a philosophical substructure.

The most remarkable thing about Pythagorean philosophy, in fact, is its concept of numbers as represented by the famous Pythagorean theorem, and this is what rightly concerns us here.

# The Principle of Number is the Principle of Existence

Aristotle tells us in *Metaphysics* (I, 5) that "the Pythagoreans, as they are called, devoted themselves to mathematics, they were the first to advance this study, and having been brought up in it they thought its principles were the principles of all things..."

One could say that the Pythagoreans were the world's first mathematics research society.

So many discoveries were made by them: the existence of prime numbers, the distinction between odd and even numbers, the graphing of a regular polyhedron, and most of the theorems of elementary geometry.

In the history of the field the earlier number systems of the ancient Egyptians and Babylonians were more arithmetic than mathematical. The preceding systems were basically methods of practical land measurement. The Pythagoreans were the first to elevate this arithmetical geodesy to the level of mathematics and geometry.

However, the Pythagoreans were not studying mathematics for the sake of the discipline itself, as is the case at today's universities. As mentioned earlier they had a higher purpose——they aspired to the eternal realm of the soul. They pursued the study of mathematics in hopes of achieving this goal, as a method of purifying their souls in an attempt to reach immortality.

The Pythagoreans contend that number is the only constant immutable factor in this ever-changing world of birth and death, of becoming and passing away. Accordingly, they claim that number is the foundation of all things, the *arche* of existence.

We examined the fact that the Milesian philosophers believed that the primary element of the world is some kind of matter, as Thales does in his assertion that "all things are water." Thales' doctrine is that the diverse phenomena of the world all arise out of this one determinate element.

The Pythagoreans make the counterclaim that the primary element is not made of matter, but is number.

Let us try to explain this a bit further.

The Pythagoreans believed, in common with the ordinary Greeks of their day, that each number was a discrete entity like a pebble. The Pythagoreans ordered units of discrete numbers into various configurations and closely contemplated the results.

What they found led them to make some fundamental suppositions. Namely, they said that number 1 is a point, number 2 is a line, number 3 is a surface, and number 4 is a solid.

The sum of the first four integers is ten $(1+2+3+4=10)$ and, as it stands, is a complete series of numbers. When these four integers are configured in order they form a triangle the Pythagoreans called the '*tetraktys*', a figure they regarded as sacred. But the '*tetraktys*' is by no means the only possible triangle. The successive ordering of integers produces an infinite number of them $(1+2=3, 1+2+3=6, 1+2+3+4=10, 1+2+3+4+5=15)$. Further, they discovered that the progression of this series of sums continues on to infinity (3, 6, 10, 15, 21, 28). They named each integer in these progressions after the basic configuration, calling them 'triangular numbers'.

In addition, they regarded the numbers produced by adding a succession of odd numbers to the number 1 (4, 9, 16, 25 and so forth) as 'square numbers'. (These square numbers configure into a square shape, from which we can immediately recognize square root relationships such as $1+3=4=2^2$, $1+3+5=9=3^2$, $1+3+5+7=16=4^2$.) In addition, they regarded the numbers produced by adding a succession of even numbers $(2+4=6, 2+4+6=12, 2+4+6+8=20$ and so forth) as 'oblong numbers'. Please refer to the following illustrations:

Representing numbers as points and shapes like this may seem a bit primitive, but the spatial study of mathematical relationships stimulated the development of geometry and, by demonstrating the magically formative and organizational capacity of numbers, finally led the Pythagoreans to their deeply held conviction that "all things are numbers."

The Pythagoreans also advanced the mathematical understanding of music. They demonstrated an extraordi-

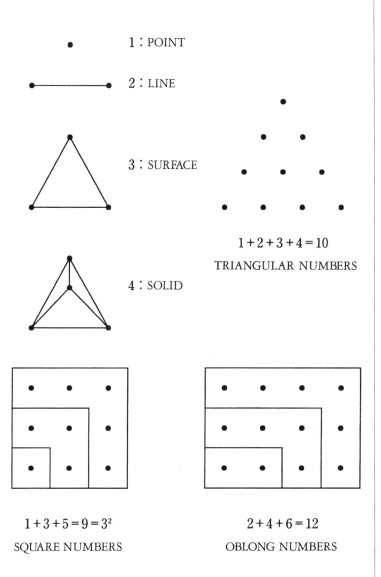

1 : POINT

2 : LINE

3 : SURFACE

$1 + 2 + 3 + 4 = 10$

TRIANGULAR NUMBERS

4 : SOLID

$1 + 3 + 5 = 9 = 3^2$

SQUARE NUMBERS

$2 + 4 + 6 = 12$

OBLONG NUMBERS

nary interest in the subject, and were the people who discovered that pitch depends on the length of the string and that intervals on the scale may be expressed by numerical ratios.

They were also the first thinkers to propose the idea that the earth is not the center of creation. The Pythagoreans were not only mathematicians, but astronomers as well.

One member of their school, Philolaus, taught that the sun, the earth, the moon, the planets, and the stars revolve round the central fire or 'hearth of the universe' in accordance with mathematical laws. Philolaus' assertion that mathematical laws control the movement of heavenly bodies was to have an enormous impact on later generations.

In addition to the belief that the heavens revolve according to mathematical principle and that the universe is an orderly sphere that has a common center, the Pythagoreans also believed that the universe produces a symphony of 'heavenly music' as it moves harmoniously through its numerically determined intervals. They claimed that ordinary people are unable to hear this music but that Pythagoras could. It does seem likely that Pythagoras was subject to this kind of mystical experience.

The insight that numbers establish the ordered integration (*harmonia*) of the universe is the core concept of Pythagorean philosophy. Again, they find that numbers are the basic element, the *arche*, of existence.

This is an idea that had a profound influence on later philosophers.

The Milesian philosophers determined the *arche* to be

some form of physical matter that exists in the natural world. The Pythagoreans declared the mentally devised concept of 'order', or 'harmony', to be theirs. Number is formed and formless. It is transcendent, connected to eternity and immortality.

The Pythagoreans may have come to this conclusion because of their religious-like faith. Religion always entails a spiritual search for something that is transcendent, eternal and immortal. By definition, when the primary element of the universe is declared to be God we have entered the realm of religion. But the Pythagoreans were philosophers, not men of religion, and they arrived at the rational decision that the primary element of the world is number. The fact that they did not establish a religious, theoretical foundation for their beliefs is not to their discredit. It simply speaks to their honor as philosophers.

The Pythagorean ideas about the nature of the *arche* are what had such an impact on the history of philosophy. The notion that there is something else here on earth besides matter is evident in Plato's theory of ideas. It also influenced the Christian theologians and later Descartes' conception of God.

# Socrates:
# The Majesty of the Setting Sun

To understand the philosophy of Socrates we have to study his life story. The enormous influence that Socrates had on human thought comes more from the way he lived, particularly the choices he made at the end of his life, than from anything he ever said. Socrates didn't write anything down so the only sources of information we have about him are second-hand. The vivid accounts of his behavior, more than the records of his ideas, eloquently describe him as someone who truly lived out the philosophy he believed in.

Socrates was born in Athens in 470 B.C., the son of Sophroniscus and Phraenarete. We know his life was ended by execution in 399 B.C., so he lived for 70 years. The records say that his mother was a midwife and his father a stoneworker. His father appears to have been a respectable citizen who left Socrates with an inheritance.

Very little is known about the first half of Socrates' life, but we do know that from his late 30's until his late 40's he served in the army during the Peloponnesian War and was sent to the front three times. He received much praise for his courage and competence.

From what we can tell, Socrates spent most of his time hanging around places like the *agora* with a group of young men, discussing the right way to live. He was so absorbed in his philosophical 'mission' that he totally ignored what was going on at home. Deciding not to professionalize his mission kept him very poor, but he always managed to somehow scrape by with the help of family money and the support of his friends. Socrates' wife, Xanthippe, was reputed to be quite a shrew, but they did have three children together and Plato indicates that she may have actually been a kindhearted, gentle woman. No matter how sweet she was, however, it's easy to imagine how she would become a nag if her husband never paid any attention to them and spent all his time away from home engaged in intense conversation with other people. One has to feel sympathy towards her.

Socrates is reported to have been a very peculiar fellow, both physically and mentally.

Apparently he was very odd looking, and supposedly he walked like a duck. But once he started to speak, his incredibly warm conviviality and brilliance were so compelling that one completely forgot his homely appearance. Socrates was physically robust and, as many commented, he had tremendous courage and endurance.

They also say that he was temperate in his habits and content with a very simple life. He wore the same garment all year long, and always went barefoot. But he loved to be with people and, when sent for, would gladly attend any festive gathering. No matter how much he drank he never got drunk. In this he was a typical gentleman of ancient Greece, delighting in the pleasures of life but never slipping into over-indulgence.

Socrates always kept his distance from politics and never held public office, but we know he was an upstanding citizen.

One of the most peculiar things about his eccentric character was that he was prone to sudden periods of deep meditative abstraction.

According to an account given by Plato, one morning Socrates was standing in the middle of a battlefield during a military campaign when he started contemplating something. Afternoon came and he was still rooted to the spot. Evening descended and the other soldiers ate their supper, but Socrates didn't move. The men took out a bedroll to him and watched to see what he would do. He didn't budge. Socrates stood there in his trance-like state the whole night long. He didn't return to himself until the next morning, when he suddenly made obeisance to the rising sun and went on his way.

One of the other strange things about Socrates was that from his youth onwards he often heard a silent 'prophetic voice' or '*daimon*' speak to him. The voice always appeared in time to warn him of danger or to stop him before he was about to make a mistake. Rather than urging him forward this way or that, it prohibited him from doing things. The voice was not just that of his own conscience. There was an otherworldly quality to it.

I find these two facets of his life particularly interesting —his spontaneous meditations and his prophetic voice.

# Socrates' Mission

Little is known for sure about Socrates' early life, but the intellectual autobiography that Plato has him relate in the *Phaedo* tells us that Socrates began his education with the study of natural philosophy, the system that tried to determine the cause of the appearance and disappearance of phenomena in the natural world. He wrestled with Parmenides' theory of 'existence', and puzzled over the paradoxes of Zeno. These earlier theories left him perplexed and discouraged about whether or not the truth really existed. Then he discovered the writings of Anaxagoras.

Socrates was excited by Anaxagoras' idea that mind (*nous*) is the primary cause of order in human society and, likewise, of law and order in the natural universe. He was profoundly disappointed when further investigation revealed that Anaxagoras' idea of mind was only that it is the material substance that set the vortex-movement of the universe in motion. He was so disheartened by this realization that he abandoned the study of natural philosophy, saying, "I have nothing to do with physical speculations."

At this point something happened that changed his life forever.

# The Delphic Oracle

Plato says in the *Apology* that this famous incident occurred "before Socrates was 35 years old."

A dear, impulsive friend of Socrates named Chaerephon approached the Delphic oracle and boldly asked the god of wisdom, Apollo, to answer the following question:

"Is there any man living who is wiser than Socrates?"

The vestal virgin delivered the answer: "No, there is no one wiser."

Socrates took the oracle very seriously. It turned out to be the turning point of his life, timed as it was with the state of his mind at the time.

We know from Plato's *Phaedo* that when Socrates was young he assiduously devoted himself to the study of natural philosophy. These various theories attempted to explain the 'how' of reality but none of them addressed the issue of 'why'. This frustrated him so much that he abandoned that line of endeavor.

Socrates says that he gave up natural philosophy because he had no aptitude for it. In fact, this seems to have been the case. The Delphic oracle may have had such a profound impact on his thinking because it came at a time when he was in a state of intellectual confusion. We know he was disillusioned with the external view of man and the universe found in the earlier philosophies. He was already turning towards the intellectual investigation of goodness and the ethical conduct of life. We can assume he was in the middle of this psychological shift from the external to the internal when he received the oracle, and that it gave him the impetus he needed to make the step forward to the study of self. He was probably wondering which way to go, and the Delphic oracle made him take a chance on this direction into his future.

Socrates' initial reaction to being confronted with the oracle was pure amazement. He didn't consider himself wise by any matter of means, so what could the gods possibly mean by this declaration?

> "What is the god saying, and what is his hidden meaning? I am only too conscious that I have no claim to wisdom, great or small; so what can he mean by asserting that I am the wisest man

in the world? He cannot be telling a lie; that would not be right for him."

Socrates puzzled about this for some time, and then went to look for people who were wiser than he in order to disprove the oracle's prophesy.

In this way, Socrates undertook the great task of visiting all kinds of purportedly brilliant individuals in order to examine their level of wisdom. He called on statesmen, poets, artisans, and the like. He discovered that, although in many people's opinions, especially their own, they appeared to be wise, in fact they were not. The politicians didn't really know anything about politics and the poets didn't really know anything about art. At least the artisans knew something about their jobs but, sadly, they didn't understand the most important things about being human.

Socrates gradually came to understand the meaning of the oracle. Apollo was using this riddle to teach him that human beings were not very wise, but any wisdom that they do have comes from recognition of their own ignorance.

Socrates' 'knowledge' or 'recognition' of his own ignorance was greater than that of anyone else, and this is why he was the wisest among men.

Realizing this, Socrates felt that he had been given a 'mission' by the gods to explain this concept to other people and to search with them for 'what every human being must know'.

This is how Socrates began to develop the method of dialogue or cross-examination (*elenchus*) for which he has become so famous.

# 'The Dialogues'

To accomplish his mission, Socrates took to the streets.

He would show up someplace, like the market, or the gymnasium, or the house of a friend, and start a dialogue with whomever he could find——a philosopher, a politician, a merchant, a craftsman, it didn't matter.

The ancient Greeks were generally known for their love of language and their passion for dialogue, but to Socrates the art of conversation went far beyond enjoyment. Talking to people was not only essential for the accomplishment of his mission; it was what gave meaning to his life.

Once Socrates began talking to someone he wouldn't let the poor fellow go until the conversation had reached some sort of resolution.

Socrates never wrote a book, and he never gave anything resembling a lecture. He was not the kind of teacher who had some pre-packaged knowledge ready to pass down to his students. He considered everyone who engaged with him in his dialogues a friend and a fellow seeker of the truth.

Plato tells us that Socrates believed himself to be like a gadfly on the rump of the huge graceful war-horse that was Athens, placed there by the gods on purpose to provide a constant irritation to the good citizens of the city so that they would stay awake. His mission was to flit about and needle each of them one by one, just like an annoying insect.

The *Apology* credits Socrates with saying: "The unexamined life is not worth living." Socrates developed his method of dialogue as a way of relentlessly examining the particulars of life.

Socrates would begin one of his dialogues by eliciting a person's opinion on some subject. He would profess total ignorance of whatever was being discussed, and listen with total attention to the other's explanation. Socrates then started a minute examination of the person's argument, picking it apart until he found something that didn't make any sense. He would continue like this until the other person was forced to admit his own ignorance. Socrates never voiced his own opinion on anything, always maintaining his ignorance about the subject at hand. This is known as Socratic 'irony'.

Socrates tried to expose the inadequacies of his partner's arguments without ever stating his own. Naturally, this could be very upsetting.

We can hear the anger in these remarks of Thrasymachos:

"I fear that Socrates here, my old friend, is feigning ignorance (*eironeia*) once again. You never answer a question. You always pretend you don't know anything when someone asks you about something, or just make up some kind of excuse to avoid giving an answer."

Similarly, Hippias complains: "You are always asking everybody so many questions and then you examine every aspect of what they have to say, but you never explain anything about what you are thinking or give an opinion when anybody asks you anything."

They were calling him to task for his irony (*eironeia*).

Irony (*eironeia*) often carries with it the implications of fraud, deceit, and concealment.

We see from these comments that some people were disgruntled when cornered by Socrates. But was he trying to fool them? The answer is definitely no. He was being unfairly criticized.

He was not being closed and dishonest.

Socrates was simply trying to uncover the truth by exposing the inconsistencies and hollowness of other people's reasoning. In particular, he was trying to debunk the arguments of the so-called Sophists, teachers of debate. He was using this technique——engaging in a dialogue about something, feigning ignorance, and eliciting exhaustive opinions——as a skillful means of exposing the weakness of their arguments.

Socrates was not consciously using 'irony' to humiliate people. With clever humor, he was seriously trying to coax the seeds of truth from the earth of men's minds. But first he had to pull out the weeds.

Socrates believed that real knowledge is not some commodity that can be handed over from a person who has it to one who does not. Rather, he was convinced that real knowledge, or wisdom, is something that is inherent within each and every one of us. Our great task is to discover it.

But it may be difficult to uncover it by oneself. Sometimes one needs outside assistance.

Employing his method of dialogue, Socrates was trying to get his 'friend' to use his own power to discover the truth for himself. Socrates used his verbal skill to get the other person to distinguish between right and wrong thinking, to separate the essential from the non-essential, and to revise and supplement one conception for another. Socrates believed that knowledge of the truth resides in everyone, and that each person has the potential to realize it for themselves. Only by realizing it through their own efforts does it become truely theirs.

Socrates used his 'dialogues' to search for the truth, and called what he did, in allusion to his mother's profession, 'midwifery' (*maieutic*).

I like to think of it as 'the cultivation of wisdom'.

So what form did Socratic dialogue take, and at what was it aiming?

Socratic dialogue took the form of a question and answer (*dialektike*), or debate. This later developed into what we call the 'dialectical method'. The aim of the dialogue was to proceed from particular examples of something to a fixed idea that represented the essential nature of that thing through the exchange of opinions and revisions to those opinions.

For example, an argument might begin with specific examples of courageous behavior and then move towards finding a fixed universal idea of the essence of 'bravery'.

Basically, then, Socrates began all of his dialogues with the question "What is this (or that)?" He subsequently endeavored to find a fixed 'definition' that answered the question. He took the question as far as it would go, because he believed that only the ultimate answer held the awareness of the truth.

As to how the definition was reached, it's fair to say that it was through a process of induction (*epagoge*).

When searching for the fixed 'definition' of something, Socrates always starts from common, concrete examples. He might choose the realm of shoemaking, or carpentry, or cow herding as the starting point for one of his philosophical arguments. Comparing one opinion on the subject to another, he works up stage by stage to build a definition that includes all of them.

The danger with this approach is falling into a competition of ideas, as did the Sophists, where one side is honor bound to beat the other. Socrates manages to avoid this, as it would have negated the whole point of the exercise, by taking opposing opinions, finding the commonality among them, and arriving, in the end, at a fixed definition that allows for the differences. Socrates believed that people are confused, but that their befuddlement contains the seeds of truth. He was convinced that these seeds would sprout once the confusion was sorted out.

# The Theory of Virtue and Wisdom

Socrates' entire life was an endless quest for the answers to the questions "What is virtue?" and "What is goodness?" He was most consumed by the search for the definition of virtue (*arete*).

In ancient Greek the word *arete* was defined as virtue, but this was not meant only in the ethical sense. It was also used to mean 'competency', as in a given skill, or 'excellence'. The virtue of carpentry, for example, is that a carpenter has the virtue (competency) to build a fine house. Further, because the carpenter needs the knowledge of certain skills to build a house, his knowledge of these skills becomes identified with the competency that his skills engender.

In general, then, virtue meant having technical knowledge in a certain area. Socrates took this definition and applied it in a broader sense to everyday life. If a carpenter with his technical skill is the one and only person who can build a proper house, it follows that someone who knows the virtue of how life should be lived is the one and only person who can live a virtuous life. As a good carpenter builds a good house, a good person leads a good life. This reasoning led Socrates to the assertion that "virtue and wisdom are the same thing."

Further, he applied the formula of identification of true knowledge and virtue to the identification of knowledge and 'goodness'.

This led Socrates to famously conclude that he who knows what is right will thereby do what is right. People can't do otherwise. Socrates believed that no one would deliberately commit evil. In other words, if someone is acting improperly it is because he or she doesn't know the truth of what is good or is somehow insufficiently aware of goodness.

We see here a predisposition towards 'happiness' that is characteristic of ancient Greece, but Socrates takes it farther and contends that, insofar as being good leads to happiness and being bad leads to unhappiness, no one who understands what evil is will ever intentionally do anything that is bad.

This axiom that "wisdom is virtue" is known as Socrates' 'paradox' and many theories were later advanced to dispute it.

A representative rebuttal comes from none other than Aristotle, who criticizes:

> (Socrates) identifies 'virtue and knowledge (*episteme*)'. He concludes, accordingly, that one who knows what is right will become a righteous person. This is like saying if you know geometry you will become a geometrician, or if you know carpentry you will become a carpenter. But this theory clearly contradicts the facts of everyday life, for we know that there are people in the world who are morally weak and who lack self-control (*akrates*) and who are led to do what they know is wrong out of desire, fear, or anger. They know what is good yet they sometimes do the opposite. Socrates does not take into account the role that the sway of the passions and moral weakness plays in human behavior.

The first thing that we need to say about this criticism is that Aristotle is incorrect in his assumption that Socrates is somehow ignorant of the human struggle against moral weakness and lack of self-control.

Xenophon (*c.* 430–*c.* 354 B.C.) tells us in his *Memorabilia* that Socrates frequently preached about the importance of the virtue of self-control, saying: "A lack of self-control causes people to become separated from their wisdom and they are thus unable to perceive the difference between right and wrong."

I suggest that Socrates had already won his own battle with moral weakness and had passed beyond the influence of the passions into a transcendent state of permanent self-control.

Herein lies the inconsistency of Aristotle's criticism. He misunderstands Socrates' use of the word wisdom, confusing it with the kind of knowledge that informs a skill such as geometry or carpentry, the kind of knowledge that one can acquire through rational understanding.

That kind of knowledge requires no moral transformation on the part of the subject. A skill like carpentry is available to anyone who has the intelligence to grasp it, whether he is good or evil, honest or not. It is like the kind of knowledge that the Sophists taught. They dealt in a wide variety of knowledge, from debating skills to grammatical theory and more, all of which were forms of learning that could be taught.

Becoming an ethical person and understanding the theory of righteousness are clearly two different things. If Socrates was talking about mere mental cognition of virtue when he talks about knowledge, then Aristotle's criticism might apply. But this is not what Socrates intends. We know this because at the same time that he claims "virtue and wisdom are one," Socrates also declares that "virtue cannot be taught."

Life teaches us that many virtuous people are not able to pass on their high standards of virtue to their children. Why not?

Because virtue isn't something you can just understand with your brain. It is something that must change your heart. Anything that can be memorized can be taught, but something that transforms your being must be found within yourself. Nobody else can impart that sort of wisdom to you.

Socrates uses 'knowing' in the sense that it is not until one becomes a virtuous person that one 'knows' virtue. If one does not act like a virtuous person, one does not know virtue. One is ignorant of it.

This is very similar to the Confucian Wang Yang-ming's doctrine of the 'unity of knowledge and action.'

Socrates speaks of 'recollection' (*anamnesis*) as true knowledge. Recollection means becoming aware of the truth dormant inside of oneself and then recognizing it as such. This is why Socrates was being completely honest when he claimed that he had nothing to teach, and why he unvaryingly maintained the position that all he could do was help others find the wisdom they contained within themselves. He could only act as a midwife.

Knowledge for Socrates means wisdom that transforms the whole personality. It entails a deep internal realization that calls forth a transformation of the soul (*psyche*). His attempts at producing insight in other people so angered certain parties that he was eventually rewarded with a death sentence.

# Pre-Birth 'Recollection' (*Anamnesis*)

The *Phaedo* is considered a representative work of

Plato's middle period. The treatise begins with a description of Socrates' trial and ends with his death.

Socrates is supposed to have said before he died: "An unjust law is still a law." He calmly accepted his death sentence and was not afraid. The *Phaedo* gives us a detailed account of the entire episode.

Bravery was not the only reason why Socrates wasn't afraid to die. It was also because he truly believed that death was the release of the soul from the physical body and, moreover, that death was the ideal realm for the philosopher.

According to Socrates, the body was not only an inconvenience to the welcome philosophical goal of attaining the truth, but if anything, a positive hindrance to speculative thinking. We can only approach the truth through pure speculation, so the purest state for the human soul is the state in which it is cut off and separated from the body, i.e., death.

We can see here the enormous influence that Pythagoras had on the development of Socratic-Platonic thought, introducing as he did the idea that the soul can break away from the body as it aspires towards an immortal eternality. And those things that the pure speculation of the soul perceives are things such as 'righteousness' and 'goodness', in other words, the 'ideas' of Socrates and Plato.

Socrates uses the word idea to mean the 'fundamental essence of something'. "What is (the fundamental existence of) that?" he asks.

Remember Parmenides' idea that existence is changeless and constant (it is).

Empedocles and Democritus later found that unchanging existence is made up of physical particles they called 'elements' and 'atoms', respectively, whereas Socrates and Plato found that it consists of 'ideas' like the entity 'righteousness' and the entity 'goodness'.

The theory of ideas says, for example, that a triangle cannot exist in the world of phenomena in its own right. What is happening when we perceive something as triangular is that we are looking through the imperfect, triangular-appearing object to the idea of triangularity that lies behind it. This is how we are able to make the discrimination that what we perceive is a triangle.

In the *Phaedo* Plato (in the voice of Socrates) explains the idea of 'equality' in the following manner.

Suppose we have two sticks that appear to be of equal length. One person looks at these two sticks and thinks: "They are equal." Where does this equality come from? Does it come from human sense perception? Another person might look at these two sticks from a different angle and think: "They are not equal." For this reason, we can say that equality does not come from sense perception. So where does the notion of equality come from? Plato says we are seeing the idea of 'equality' that lies behind the two sticks.

A person makes the discrimination that two sticks are equal or not by recollecting the idea of 'equality'.

And from where does the person recollect it?

Plato's answer is that one recollects it from before one was born.

# Idea and Logos

The Greek word *'idea'* is the root of the words idea and ideology in European languages. But Plato uses it to mean much more than simply what we have inside of our heads.

Just as the Pythagoreans found number to exist before natural order, Plato finds that ideas exist before they appear in our minds, that they have an objective existence. In this way of thinking, ideas, reminiscent of Parmenides, are changeless and indivisible. In short, the idea is the *arche* of reality.

Plato was the first philosopher to state that 'idea' pre-exists 'judgement' or, in more contemporary terminology, that conception precedes discrimination. If we don't know the word (concept) for dog and we see little Spot sitting there in front of us, we can't make the discrimination that Spot is a dog.

But for Plato, as well as Greek philosophy in general, the fact that an idea of something (such as equality) exists before one can make a judgement about it is not just about discrimination (recognition). It involves many other issues, such as the immortality of the soul, the permanency of existence, the temporality of the body, etc.

Plato contends that we are able to recollect ideas because we knew them before we were born, but because the soul is imprisoned within the human body we are unable to see them directly in their own right. We have forgotten what we used to know of the realm of ideas.

However, when we perceive something here in the phenomenological world that reminds us of what we used to know, our memory is jogged and we are able to recollect it. This is how we recognize the truth.

Plato (and Socrates) claim anything our senses perceive as 'equal' cannot in reality be 'equal' because sense perception differs from person to person. Sense perception is what causes us to think that two things that are not equal are equal and vice versa.

Plato says that anything perceptible to the senses "is intended to be like something else (equal), but it falls short and cannot be really like it, only a poor imitation." The senses are imperfect, but as we utilize them from the moment of our birth it is impossible for us to divorce ourselves from their functioning. Philosophy may be training for pure speculation, but there has never been a person who existed as pure philosophy. Yet we are able to (purely) recollect an idea such as that of equality. From where can we recollect it, since we live in this world and thus cannot unshackle ourselves from the restrictions of our senses?

Plato answers that we are recollecting knowledge that we obtained before we were born. As long as the soul is connected to something permanent and immortal it can not vanish, even when it is separated from the body at the time of death.

This assumption is the foundation of Socrates' conviction about the immortality of the soul that he voiced as he was facing his death. For the philosopher, death is perforce a welcome thing.

For it is through death that the soul returns to the realm of ideas, its ancestral home and its eternal abode.

After Pythagoras entered the picture, the object of philosophical inquiry became something that was no longer visible to the human eye. Then Parmenides added the notion that the nature of true existence is one, unchanging and indivisible.

Adopting and continuing this lineage, Socrates and Plato found that ideas are what lie at the basis of the visible, phenomenological world. Ideas are changeless and are the *arche* of the universe. In this sense their idea is no different from the 'number' of Pythagoras, but the 'idea' is something we can explore more clearly with words (*logos*).

Philosophy, which began with the search for a permanent reality underlying the diversity of the natural world, has now discovered *logos*.

By definition, *logos* is not something that could have arisen after the birth of man. It had to exist before. First there is *logos* (idea), and then the world was born.

The *Gospel According to St. John* begins with the famous passage:

"In the beginning was the Word (*logos*), and the Word was with God, and the Word was God."

The original Greek term translated here as 'word' is *logos*, but there are many other ways it can be rendered, such as 'act' or 'light'. *Logos* has a wide breadth of meaning, containing within itself the notions that truth resides within words as words are the light that show us that truth, and that words contain a mystical power to speak to us.

St. John was one of the Twelve Apostles. He authored his Gospel in Asia Minor near the end of the first century. It continues:

"And the Word was made flesh (*Jesus Christ*), and dwelt among us (and we beheld [Jesus'] glory, the glory as of the only begotten of the Father), full of grace and truth."

Socrates was born in 470 B.C. and Plato in 427 B.C. St. John wrote these words at the end of the first century, so he lived about 500 years after them.

We see how useful Greek philosophy was to the establishment of Christianity.

# The Voice of the *Daimon* is the Voice of Idea

There is another important thing that we learn from the death of Socrates.

Socrates was sentenced to death by a court of law. Records tell us that the tribunal never expected the whole thing to go that far, but Socrates clung to his mission so stubbornly during his testimony that he brought the court to a point where they could not back off. In the end, the jury gave him the death penalty.

Under Athenian custom Socrates should have been executed within 24 hours of his sentence, but due to happenstance, he was left lingering in prison for about a month. During that time, friends of his like Crito made elaborate plans for him to escape and go into exile, but he refused to agree to them. Instead, he tranquilly drank the cup of hemlock in the late spring of 399 B.C.

Death was not something strange and foreign to

Socrates. Instead, Socrates viewed death as a return to the realm of ideas, to the home of the soul, to the field of eternity. Perhaps he longed for it as one does the land of one's birth. He does tell us certain things.

He talks about the voice of the *daimon* that often told him how to behave.

When Socrates receives his verdict, he says: "Now something has happened to me, as you can see, which might be thought and is commonly considered to be a supreme calamity; yet...not at any point...did the divine sign oppose me."

Indeed, one would ordinarily think that receiving the death penalty was a disaster. It's hard to imagine anything worse. But Socrates concludes that it is a blessing. His paradoxical conviction is based on the fact that the *daimon* did not oppose him. We can't help but think that, in his *daimon*, Socrates was connected to some kind of higher truth.

The voice visited him often over the course of his lifetime. It never came to urge him forward, but always appeared to show him the truth by stopping him from making a mistake.

In the long religious tradition of Greece, a *daimon* was originally not a god but an intermediary between god and man who emanated from a supra-human, spiritual dimension. In Diotima's dialogue in the *Symposium*, Plato speaks of Eros as a great *daimon* who exists between the human and the divine, carrying supplications from man to the gods and conveying commands from the gods back to man.

However, it appears that Socrates' *daimon* was not associated with any particular religion.

Personally, this is what I think.

I think that, in Socrates' case, the voice of the *daimon* was none other than the voice of idea.

I also think it is probable that Socrates received his conception of idea from the *daimon*.

And, similarly, I believe that the prophetic voice led him to the idea that conceptualization precedes discrimination.

Socrates lived for more than 70 years, and spent his lifetime as an outstanding philosopher. He was able to live an error-free life because he heard the voice of his *daimon* and heeded what it had to say.

There is no reason to suspect that, in the end, the *daimon* was mistaken in not trying to prohibit his behavior.

If Socrates had escaped from prison, would his reputation ever have reached its present magnitude? The *daimon* was right not to speak.

Socrates was not some fanatic who heard disembodied voices, nor was he mentally ill. His convictions about his *daimon* were sure and certain, but I don't think he believed that the *daimon* was a god or an intermediary between the gods and man.

As a philosopher, I expect that he was more closely connected to the concept of ideas than to that of the gods.

And his concept of ideas is what connects him to Plato.

# From Socrates to Plato

Plato's philosophy is 'the theory of ideas'.

Or, at the very least, we can say that 'the theory of ideas' is central to Platonic philosophy.

Before we can attempt to understand this philosophy, we need to realize that the meaning of the word 'idea' has come to mean something completely different than it did in Plato's time. In short, today the word idea basically means 'concept', but the origin of idea (or *eidos*) comes from the verb *idein* (to see), in the sense that we 'see' the 'true shape' or 'absolute form' of something with the mental eye.

What kind of entity is the absolute form, this idea (or *eidos*) of something?

Let us take a triangle, for example. We accept as fact that the sum of the interior angles of a triangle equals the sum of two right angles.

But what are we really talking about?

Is it about the triangle perceived by our senses?

No matter how skillful we are at drawing, any triangle we can configure will do no more than approximate this definition, while the triangle that is the subject of geometric study is a figure that does satisfy it. And while our perceptions inform us that there are different kinds of triangles, such as equilateral triangles and right triangles, the geometric definition of a triangle, that the internal angles equal two right angles, is a general definition of triangles that covers all the particulars. Even if the triangle of our perceptions changes or should disappear, the geometric triangle remains universal and eternal.

In other words, the geometric triangle is a universal (generalized), perfect triangle, fixed and imperishable, one that transcends the individual, imperfect, changeable triangle of our sensory experience. The geometric triangle is the absolute form of the triangle (its *eidos*, or idea), and we are able to 'see' through the particular triangles of our everyday experience to this idea with our 'eyes of reason'.

The idea (or *eidos*) of triangle is what geometry studies, and it is the standard by which we judge the perfection of any graphic representation of a triangle that we can create.

Now, when Plato explains the reality of the idea he prefers to illustrate his argument with examples like morality or beauty.

We perceive things in relative terms; we judge a certain behavior as being more or less correct, we judge a certain thing as being more or less beautiful. In making these judgements, we compare the thing in question against some kind of standard. In this case, we see through what we perceive as being correct or beautiful to a perfect, ideal form of 'righteousness' or 'beauty' (in other words, the *eidos*, or idea, of righteousness or beauty). (If we didn't, we wouldn't be able to judge anything at all.)

As to the difference between the two philosophers' concepts of the idea, Socrates begins by taking particular examples of virtuous behavior (such as courageous or righteous acts). He uses these to establish a fixed definition (of bravery or righteousness) and then pushes the argument towards a clear understanding of the essence of this 'virtue'. Plato takes these perfect virtues of Socrates and finds them to be actual existences (as ideas).

We can think about it this way.

The 'theory of ideas' originated with Socrates and was perfected by Plato.

Socrates martyred himself for this theory.

His death was like the majestic orb of the glowing sun setting over the horizon.

Socrates had a *daimon* that spoke to him, a voice from the realm of ideas. He complied with the messages he was given, and resigned himself calmly to his fate.

Socrates devoted his life to the actualization of the idea.

And this is what Plato inherited from him.

# The Practice of Death

There is a famous quote from Plato that says philosophy is the 'practice of death' (*meditatio mortis*).

Let us excerpt the relevant passages from the *Phaedo*:

'So it is clear first of all in the case of physical pleasure that the philosopher frees his soul from association with the body (so far as is possible) in a way that other men don't?' (65a)

'All these considerations,' said Socrates, 'must surely prompt serious philosophers to review the position in some way as this. "It looks as if it's a side-track, to divert us——and reason along with us ——in our investigation. So long as we keep to the body and our soul is contaminated with this imperfection, there is no chance of our ever attaining satisfactorily to our object, which we assert to be Truth. In the first place, the body provides us with innumerable distractions in the pursuit of its necessary sustenance, and any diseases, which attack us, hinder our quest for reality. Besides, the body fills us with loves and desires and fears and all sorts of fancies and a great deal of nonsense, with the result that we literally never get an opportunity to think at all about anything. Wars and revolutions and battles, you see, are due simply and solely to the body and its desires. All wars are undertaken for the acquisition of wealth; and the reason why we have to acquire wealth is the body, because we are slaves in its service. That is why, on all these accounts, we have so little time for philosophy.'" (66b • c)

'Is not what we call death a freeing and separation of soul from body?'

'Certainly.'

'And the desire to free the soul is found chiefly, or rather only in the true philosopher ; in fact the philosopher's occupation consists precisely in the freeing and separation of soul from body. Isn't that so?'

'Apparently.'

'Well, then, as I said at the beginning, if a man has trained himself throughout his life to live in a state as close as possible to death, would it not be ridiculous for him to be distressed when death comes to him?'

'It would, of course.'(67 d • e)

'But the soul, the invisible part, which goes away to a place that is, like itself, glorious, pure, and invisible——the true Hades or unseen world ——into the presence of the good and wise God (where, if God so wills, my soul must shortly go) ——will it, if its very nature is such as I have described, be blown to bits and destroyed at the moment of its release from the body, as most people claim?'

'The truth is much more like this: if at its release the soul is pure and does not drag along with it any trace of the body, because it has never willingly associated with it in life; if it has shunned it and isolated itself because that is what it always practices——I mean doing philosophy in the right way and really getting used to facing death calmly: wouldn't you call this "practicing death"?'

'Most decidedly.' (80e • 81a)

Here Plato contends that, insofar as we are restricted by the conditions of life here on earth, we are unable to attain the wisdom that is the goal of philosophy. We can only attain true, fundamental wisdom through the pure soul that is obtained when we are released completely from these limitations.

Having come this far in our discussion, we begin to see an element that is important in our comparison of the

wisdom of Greek philosophy and the wisdom of Gotama
Buddha. Dr. Tozu focuses on it in the following passage:

We should note here that all the bonds that
restrict the soul are somehow related to the physical body. So the only way for the soul to be
completely free to attain its own selfhood is to find
release from the physical body. And this, of course,
means death. Hence death becomes a requirement
for the purity of soul necessary to perceive true
wisdom. From here, Plato maintains, the soul is
able to enter its original, or eternal, life.

Plato is not conjuring some vague paean to
death the way one might glorify life. Rather, he is
saying that the ultimate state to which philosophy
aspires must be that of death. This raises a very
interesting problem, for, if the ultimate goal of
philosophy turns out to be death, it would seem
that the question of philosophy's utility for this life
becomes meaningless.

When we question the usefulness of philosophy we are asking what relevance it has to our
present lives. But now death, the negative turning
point of this life, becomes the goal.

Insofar as this is so, even if philosophy should
prove to have some utility in this life, such usefulness no longer pertains to its main purpose.

Philosophy may have no real relevancy to this
life and, in fact, therein may lie its true value. We
must strive to keep this the way it is.

This position transforms philosophy into something that, rather than being connected to real life, teaches us how to prepare for death. This doesn't mean it teaches us how to make mental arrangements for meeting death, but, rather, that it encourages us to make our best efforts at releasing the soul from its association with the living physical body while living in this reality, in order to maintain it in a state of self-contained purity. We need to bring death from the other shore onto this one. Although it is not actual death, we should struggle to situate the consciousness of death within this present life. In this way, philosophy is a 'rehearsal' of death, and, as such, can be viewed as a path that leads beyond worldly affairs or a pathway to liberation that brings about conclusive purification of the soul.

I find Dr. Tozu's comments fascinating.

Particularly interesting is his use of the terms 'path that leads beyond worldly affairs' and 'pathway to liberation' as metaphors for aspects of the philosophical doctrines of Socrates and Plato.

Later we will look at how these relate to the path that Gotama Buddha took in his search for wisdom.

# Aristotle's *Metaphysics*

*Philosophia* began in the sixth century B.C. as the intellectual expression of the distinctively Greek desire 'to acquire knowledge for knowledge's sake'. The discipline made great advances under Socrates and Plato, and attained its fullest awakening in the work of Aristotle. We see this awakening first in the results of Aristotle's scholarly research and reflections and later in his system of knowledge classification.

Aristotle's scholarly investigations resulted in what we know as 'logic', and his system of classifications created the distinction between what we now call philosophy and the other (specialized) sciences. Up until his time, philosophy and the sciences were considered a single branch of knowledge.

Aristotle maintains that philosophy and science are the organization of the knowledge that man discovers in his attempt to satisfy his need to know without seeking any practical benefit.

His *Metaphysics* begins with the line "All men by nature desire to know," reflecting the proposition that (then as now) the search for knowledge originates from man's sense of wonder. Philosophy and the other sciences cannot exist without this desire to find the pure truth.

The first major classification that Aristotle devised to organize knowledge into categories has to do with whether it was gained for speculative, *theoretical* reasons or for *practical* ones.

In the first place, the reasons for gaining the knowledge are different. Basically, theoretical scholarship is performed for the satisfaction of the knowledge gained, whereas practical discipline is also performed in order to use whatever is learned to improve a given situation. Ethics and political science, for example, both try to understand the true nature of man not only for knowledge's sake but to help build the proper foundations for education and politics.

Secondly, the objects of the two are different. Practical learning focuses on matters and relationships that are subject to the influence of human will, whereas theoretical learning studies 'things that are', matters and relationships that function independently of man's will. Hence 'matters of certainty' are the foci of theoretical studies and 'matters of chance' are those of the practical disciplines.

Aristotle classified theoretical learning into three subdivisions: first philosophy, mathematics, and natural philosophy (*physica*).

In Aristotle's anthology of treatises *Metaphysics* (*Metaphysica*), so named because it was compiled after (*meta*) his *Physics* (*Physica*), he defines 'first philosophy' as that which studies existence as existence, or, in his own words, *being qua being*. First philosophy thus investigates the universal characteristics of existence itself.

Further, Aristotle argues, because we can best see the universal qualities of existence in the things that cause phenomenological existence, first philosophy studies the qualities of these causes as well. Aristotle asserts that God is the primary cause of all things, and this is the assertion that carries first philosophy to its summit. It is also the one that brings first philosophy into the realm of theology.

In any event, it is clear that Aristotle's *Metaphysics* is aiming towards God. Chapter 12 is devoted exclusively to a discussion of this topic. Aristotle characterizes God as the First Form (*eidos*), the Supreme Cause (Ultimate Goal), and the First Mover. As the First Mover, God sets everything else in motion without Himself being moved, hence He is also known as the Unmoved Mover.

This proposition that God is inexhaustible Existence possessing infinite potential to cause movement in others while maintaining absolute stillness of Self is an outstanding theoretical explanation of His existence.

It is an assertion that was later appropriated by the Christian theologians as a basic tenet of Christian doctrine.


So, how are we doing?

I have tried to summarize the basic suppositions of some of the leading thinkers of Greek philosophy. I wish I could introduce more of them, but then this book would be unending. And, as I mentioned before, this is not meant to be a history or an outline of Western philosophy. I merely wanted to explore what it means to search for wisdom and how one goes about it.

I tried to focus the discussion by choosing philosophers whose theories seem to bear some kind of relationship to the wisdom realized by Shakyamuni Buddha.

I certainly don't pretend to claim a mastery of the field, but I hope I have been successful in shedding light on a small part of it. I hope I have been able to give you some idea of what the love and search for wisdom meant to the ancient Greek philosophers.

(Part I relies on the following sources: *Seiyo Kodai Chusei Tetsugakushi* [The History of Ancient and Medieval Western Philosophy], *Tekisutobukku Seiyo Tetsugakushi* [A Textbook of Western Philosophy], and *Irasuto Seiyo Tetsugakushi* [An Illustrated History of Western Philosophy].)

Part II

# Agon Buddhism:
# The Religion of Wisdom

# The Wisdom of Gotama Buddha

Now we are ready to ask the question "What kind of wisdom was the Buddha searching for?"

As many of you already know, when Gotama was 29 years old he renounced his position as crown prince, left his wife and child, and became a wandering monk.

What made him leave home?

According to the *Mahashihanada Sutta* of the *Majjhima Nikaya* he left home to search for Noble Wisdom.

The sutra also tells us that only by acquiring this Noble Wisdom can one attain Nibbana (nirvana) and achieve the cessation of all suffering.

Again, in the sutra *The Noble Search*, found in the *Majjhima Nikaya*, the Buddha says: "I went forth from the home life into homelessness to seek the birthless, unageing, unailing, deathless, sorrowless, and undefiled supreme security from bondage, Nibbana." In other words, he went to search for the wisdom that would lead him to nirvana.

What made him decide to search for this wisdom?

It was because he felt an awesome sense of wonder.

As Aristotle says in the beginning of *Metaphysics*, "All men by nature desire to know." As we have seen, philosophy begins with this sense of wonder, and, as Aristotle asserts, real philosophy or science cannot emerge without a genuine desire to discover the truth.

Gotama felt an overwhelming sense of wonder when he first understood that all human beings are destined to encounter old age, sickness, and death.

He hadn't been aware of these things.

His father the king sheltered him from this knowledge by prohibiting everyone around him from speaking of such matters, for the king feared the truth would awaken unwanted religious sentiments in Gotama's mind.

Then one day the prince managed to journey outside the palace walls. There he chanced to encounter a man who was old, one who was sick, and one who was dead.

He understood for the first time the truth of aging, sickness, and death.

This information hit him like a thunderbolt out of the blue. He realized that he, too, would have to face the realities of life. He was awestruck: "What is this life we are living, in which we have to bear the suffering of never knowing when we will be attacked by sickness or death, this life where we get older day by day?"

The more Gotama pondered, the greater his fear and amazement grew.

Resolving the question of suffering (birth, age, sickness, and death) became the most important thing in Gotama's life. Without this resolution, his life would have no meaning.

It would seem that the Buddha's motivation to discover the truth was different from the 'love of wisdom' that characterized the more leisurely approach taken by the ancient Greeks. Gotama was so desperate to find wisdom that he abandoned his home life to do so.

Because the starting point of the journey is so different, the wisdom that the Buddha will find is bound to be different from that of the Greek philosophers.

So, what is this thing called nirvana? What is he talking

about?

And why does attaining nirvana resolve suffering? This sounds like something that anyone would want to know.

We are never given a straight answer, however.

While it is clear that the Buddha attained nirvana, he never defines it precisely or tells us what it's like.

Indian philosophy uses the term 'liberation' to refer the state of existence in which one has achieved separation from human suffering. Buddhism also uses the term nirvana to refer to this state.

The word itself is Sanskrit (Nibbana is the Pali reading). In Chinese and Japanese it is written *Nehan* (涅槃) or *Naion* (泥洹). These characters may be loosely translated to mean something equivalent to the 'non-action' of Taoism.

Buddhist scholars have long debated the meaning of the word. They define it variously as 'the pacification of agitation' or 'tranquil settling', but 'extinguishing the flame' or 'having extinguished the flame' are generally held to be closer to the true sense. Entering nirvana is often likened to dousing a fire with water.

Ashvaghosha, who lived in the first century, comments in his work *Saundarananda* that entering nirvana is like the extinction of a flame. He tells us that a person's afflictions, or taints (*klesha*), completely vanish and disappear, just like the flame of a lantern that has run out of oil. But what is it that actually disappears? He never makes this explicit. We are just given the impression that the individual somehow takes on a brand new, separate existence.

We learn something about nirvana from the way the Buddha's disciples describe it in the sutras. For example:

"The bhikkhu who detaches himself from the worldly

passions and realizes wisdom attains the state of Tranquillity (nirvana) of no death, no aging, and no cessation." (*Suttanipata*)

"Tranquillity (nirvana) is not an illusion. All sages know this to be true. And realizing this truth, they stop craving pleasure and achieve peacefulness." (*Suttanipata*)

Similar descriptions appear here and there throughout the Buddhist scriptures.

The Buddha mentions nirvana when he responds to questions about it from his disciples. He says:

"All those who would be venerable, believe in the right Dhamma of entering and abiding in Tranquillity (nirvana), strive and be wise, listen carefully to the teachings, and you will finally achieve true wisdom." (*Suttanipata*)

And in response to the question "On the cessation of what depends Tranquillity (nirvana)?" the Buddha answers:

"Tranquillity (nirvana) is the cessation of craving (*tanha*)."

In a further instance, one time an old man named Pingiya came to see the Buddha and asked him:

"I am old, and weak, and my appearance has withered. My vision is dim; my hearing is dull. Please help me resolve my confusion before I die. I beg you to teach me how to extinguish birth and decrepitude while in this very life. This is what I want to know." (*Suttanipata*)

Pingiya wants to know how to attain Tranquillity (nirvana).

The Buddha answered:

"Pingiya, Friend, people become decrepit because they have material form and because they have material form idle people suffer (from sickness and the like). Because of this, do not be idle, abandon your material form, and return not to this state of existence."

The Buddha counsels Pingiya to free himself from the yoke of physical reality. Pingiya then asks him how to do this, and the Buddha answers:

"Pingiya, Friend, suffering arises because men are consumed with craving (*tanha*) and that is why they grow old, so I encourage you to be diligent, abandon craving, and return not again to this confused state of existence." (*Suttanipata*)

In short, the Buddha advocates renouncing attachment to the physical body.

So the Buddha does, in a way, answer questions about nirvana but never offers a precise definition of what it actually is. He is willing to discuss how to attain nirvana, the path to reach it, but he doesn't tell us anything about the state itself.

# Nirvana According to *The Questions of King Milinda*

Dr. B. Bhattacharyya comments on this matter in his book *An Introduction to Buddhist Esoterism* (1932):

Buddha was himself satisfied when the truth of Nirvāṇa dawned on him: this was a loftier doctrine than any the leading Sāṅkhya philosophers of his age taught. But did he define Nirvāṇa? No.

Whenever questioned, his usual answer was: 'You should first realize Nirvāṇa and then you can know what it is. You need not know that even. The attainment of Nirvāṇa will give you freedom from births and rebirths, which means emancipation.'

Buddhists have long pondered the meaning of the Buddha's 'mystic silence' (as Bhattacharyya calls it).

Various arguments have been put forward by many generations of scholars and various theories have been proposed to account for it. The fundamental error in Mahayana thought arose from the misreading of the word nirvana, something I'll have to go into on another occasion. (Please refer to my book *Agon Buddhism as the Source of Shamatha* [*Tranquillity*] *and Vipashyana* [*Insight*] for more on this topic.)

How do the sutras define it?

Here is a passage from the *Ariyapariyesana Sutta (The Noble Search)*, sutra 26 of the *Majjhima Nikaya*, in which the Buddha speaks of attaining Nirvana:

Then, bhikkus, being myself subject to ageing, having understood the danger in what is subject to ageing, seeking the unageing supreme security from bondage, Nibbana, I attained the unageing supreme security from bondage, Nibbana; being myself subject to sickness... I attained the unailing supreme security from bondage, Nibbana; being myself subject to death... I attained the deathless supreme security from bondage, Nibbana; being myself subject to sorrow... I attained the sorrowless supreme security from bondage, Nibbana; being myself subject to defilement... I attained the undefiled supreme security from bondage, Nibbana.

The Chinese translators expanded this single word into a term whose characters translate as:
'the-unailing-unageing-deathless-sorrowless-undefiled-supreme-security-from-bondage-Nirvana'
How are we to understand the meaning of the word from this translation?

The translators could find no other way to express it.

To get some help, we turn to a renowned conversation between the Ionian Greek King Milinda and the Indian pundit Nagasena on the topic of nirvana that took place in the second century. This discussion took the form of questions from the king and eloquent answers from the monk in response. It was written down as a sutra called *The Questions of King Milinda*. I will excerpt a relevant passage of it here.

'Venerable Nagasena, this Nirvana that you are always talking of——can you make clear by metaphor, or explanation, or reason, or argument, the form, or figure, or duration, or measure of it?'

'Nirvana, O king, has nothing similar to it. By no metaphor, or explanation, or reason, or argument can its form, or figure, or duration, or measure be made clear.'

'That I cannot believe, Nagasena,——that of Nirvana, which really after all is a condition that exists, it should be so impossible to make us understand either the form, or figure, or duration, or measure! Give me some explanation of this.'

'As impossible as it is, O king, to tell the measure of the water in the sea, or the number of the creatures dwelling therein, though after all the sea exists, so impossible is it in any of the ways you suggest to tell the form, or figure, or duration, or measure of Nirvana, though after all it is a condition that does exist. And even, O king, if one of magical powers, master over mind, were to be able to count the water and the creatures in the sea, even he could not tell the form or the figure, the duration or the measure of Nirvana.'

'Though there is nothing as to its form which can be so explained, there is something, O King, as to its qualities which can.'

'O happy word, Nagasena! Speak then, quickly, that I may have an explanation of even one point in the characteristics of Nirvana. Appease the fever of my heart. Allay it by the cool sweet breezes of your words!'

'There is one quality of the lotus, O king, inherent in Nirvana, and two qualities of water, and three of medicine, and four of the ocean, and five of food, and ten of space, and three of the wish-conferring gem, and three of red sandal wood, and three of the froth of ghee, and five of a mountain peak.'

'As the lotus, O king, is untarnished by the water, so is Nirvana untarnished by any evil dispositions. This is the one quality of the lotus inherent in Nirvana.'

'As water, O king, is cool and assuages heat, so also is Nirvana cool, and assuages the fever arising from all evil dispositions. This is the first quality of water inherent in Nirvana. And again, O king, as water allays the thirst of men and beasts when they are exhausted and anxious, craving for drink, and tormented by thirst, so does Nirvana allay the thirst of the craving after lusts, the craving after future life, and the craving after worldly prosperity. This is the second quality of water inherent in Nirvana.'

'As medicine, O king, is the refuge of beings tormented by poison, so is Nirvana the refuge of beings tormented with the poison of evil dispositions. This is the first quality of medicine inherent in Nirvana. And again, O king, as medicine puts an end to diseases, so does Nirvana put an end to grief. This is the second quality of medicine inherent in Nirvana. And again, O king, as medicine is ambrosia, so also is Nirvana ambrosia. This is the third quality of medicine inherent in Nirvana.'

'As the ocean, O king, is free from (empty of) corpses, so also is Nirvana free from (empty of) the dead bodies of all evil dispositions. This, O king, is the first quality of the ocean inherent in Nirvana. And again, O king, as the ocean is mighty and boundless, and fills not with all the rivers that flow in to it; so is Nirvana mighty and boundless, and fills not with all beings (who enter in to it).

This is the second quality of the ocean inherent in Nirvana. And again, O king, as the ocean is the abode of mighty creatures, so is Nirvana the abode of great men——Arhats, in whom the Great Evils and all stains have been destroyed, endowed with power, masters of themselves. This is the third quality of the ocean inherent in Nirvana. And again, O king, as the ocean is all in blossom, as it were, with the innumerable and various and fine flowers of the ripple of its waves, so is Nirvana all in blossom, as it were, with the innumerable and various and fine flowers of purity, of knowledge, and of emancipation. This is the fourth quality of the ocean inherent in Nirvana.'

'As food, O king, is the support of the life of all beings, so is Nirvana, when it has been realized, the support of life, for it puts an end to old age and death. This is the first quality of food inherent in Nirvana. And again, O king, as food increases the strength of all beings, so does Nirvana, when it has been realized, increase the power of Iddhi of all beings. This is the second quality of food inherent in Nirvana. And again, O king, as food is the source of the beauty of all beings, so is Nirvana, when it has been realized, the source to all beings of the beauty of holiness. This is the third quality of food inherent in Nirvana. And again, O king, as food puts a stop to suffering in all beings, so does Nirvana, when it has been realized, put a stop in all beings to the suffering arising from every evil disposition. This is the fourth quality of food inherent in Nirvana. And again, O king, as food overcomes in all beings the weakness of hunger, so does Nirvana, when it has been realized, overcome in all beings the weakness which arises from hunger and every sort of pain. This is the fifth quality of food inherent in Nirvana.'

'As space, O king, neither is born nor grows old, neither dies nor passes away nor is reborn (has a future life to spring up into), as it is incomprehensible, cannot be carried off by thieves, rests on nothing, is the sphere in which birds fly, is unobstructed, and is infinite; so, O king, Nirvana is not born, neither does it grow old, it dies not, it passes not away, it has no rebirth (no future life to spring up into), it is unconquerable, thieves carry it not off, it is not attached to anything, it is the sphere in which Arahats move, nothing can obstruct it, and it is infinite. These are ten qualities of space inherent in Nirvana.'

'As the wishing-gem, O king, satisfies every desire, so also does Nirvana. This is the first quality of the wishing-gem inherent in Nirvana. And again, O king, as the wishing-gem causes delight, so also does Nirvana. This is the second quality of the wishing-gem inherent in Nirvana. And again, O king, as the wishing-gem is full of luster, so also is Nirvana. This is the third quality of the wishing-gem inherent in Nirvana.'

'As red sandal wood, O king, is hard to get, so is Nirvana hard to attain to. This is the first quality of red sandal wood inherent in Nirvana. And again, O king, as red sandal wood is unequaled in the beauty of its perfume, so is Nirvana. This is the second quality of red sandal wood inherent in Nirvana. And again, O king, as red sandal wood is praised by all the good, so is Nirvana praised by all the Noble Ones. This is the third quality of red sandal wood inherent in Nirvana.'

'As ghee is beautiful in color, O king, so also is Nirvana beautiful in righteousness. This is the first quality of ghee inherent in Nirvana. And again, O king, as ghee has a pleasant perfume, so also has Nirvana the pleasant perfume of righteousness. This is the second quality of ghee inherent in Nirvana. And again, O king, as ghee has a pleasant taste, so also has Nirvana. This is the third quality of ghee inherent in Nirvana.'

'As a mountain peak is very lofty, so also is Nirvana very exalted. This is the first quality of a mountain peak inherent in Nirvana. And again, O king, as a mountain peak is immoveable, so also is Nirvana. This is the second quality of a mountain peak inherent in Nirvana. And again, O king, as a mountain peak is inaccessible, so also is Nirvana inaccessible to all evil dispositions. This is the third quality of a mountain peak inherent in Nirvana. And again, O king, as a mountain peak is a place where no plants can grow, so also is Nirvana a condition in which no evil dispositions can grow. This is the fourth quality of a mountain peak inherent in Nirvana. And again, O king, as a mountain peak is free alike from desire to please and from resentment, so also is Nirvana. This is the fifth quality of a mountain peak inherent in Nirvana.'

'Very good, Nagasena! That is so, and I accept it as you say.'


This is quite an explanation!

In beautiful, poetic phrases, the pundit Nagasena's luxurious words entranced King Milinda. While still under their spell, I imagine the king thought he understood it all very clearly. But I can't help wondering if later on, after he had time to think about it, the king was no longer so sure what the pundit was trying to say.

Parenthetically, there is another question the king asks Nagasena that is of interest here.

Apparently, the king has heard that it takes an enormous amount of effort and a great deal of discipline to attain nirvana. So he wants to be assured that, after enduring so much hardship, reaching nirvana will be worth it. How do we know that nirvana is really such an ideal state?

Nagasena makes the following retort:

'Now what do you think, O king? Do those whose hands and feet have not been cut off know how sad a thing it is to have them cut off?'

'Yes, Sir, that they know.'

'But how do they know it?'

'Well, by hearing the sound of the lamentation of those whose hands and feet have been cut off, they know it.'

'Just so, great king, it is by hearing the glad words of those who have seen Nirvana, that they who have not received it know how happy a state it is.'

'Very good, Nagasena!'

# The Buddha's 'Mystic Silence'

Why do we suppose that the Buddha, who told his disciples that they had to attain nirvana, refused to explain to them what it really is?

As noted, Dr. Bhattacharyya calls this omission 'mystic'.

But it doesn't strike me as being all that enigmatic.

Didn't we see something very similar to this situation when we were discussing Socrates? As I noted in Part I:

Socrates believed that real knowledge is not some commodity that can be handed over from a person who has it to one who does not. Rather, he was convinced that wisdom is something that inherently exists within each and every one of us. Our great task is to discover it.

But it may be difficult to uncover it by oneself. Sometimes one needs outside assistance.

Employing his method of dialogue, Socrates

was trying to get his 'friend' to use his own power to discover the truth for himself. Socrates used his verbal skill to get the other person to distinguish between right and wrong thinking, to separate the essential from the non-essential, and to revise and supplement one conception for another. Socrates believed that knowledge of the truth resides in everyone, and that each person has the potential to realize it for themselves. Only by realizing it through their own efforts does it become truly theirs.

Similarly, the ability to give someone information about nirvana doesn't mean one is able to convey the experience of the actuality of nirvana. How much truer this must be for the wisdom of nirvana. That wisdom is something that you have to realize by yourself.

It is no wonder that the Buddha refused to give a direct answer.

# The Spiritual Practices by which the Buddha Attained Wisdom

The first thing Gotama Buddha did when he went out in search of wisdom was to visit the ascetic Alara Kalama and request teachings. Alara was a well-known sage of the time who had over 700 disciples.

The Buddha recounts their meeting in sutra 26 of the

*Majjhima Nikaya, The Noble Search*:

"Having gone forth, bhikkhus, in search of what is wholesome, seeking the supreme state of sublime peace, I went to Alara Kalama and said to him: 'Friend Kalama, I want to lead the holy life in this Dhamma and Discipline.' Alara Kalama replied: 'The venerable one may stay here. This Dhamma is such that a wise man can soon enter upon and abide in it, realizing for himself through direct knowledge his own teacher's doctrine.' I soon quickly learned that Dhamma. As far as mere lip-reciting and rehearsal of his teaching went, I could speak with knowledge and assurance, and I claimed, 'I know and see'——and there were others who did likewise.

"I considered: 'It is not through mere faith alone that Alara Kalama declares: "By realizing for myself with direct knowledge, I enter upon and abide in this Dhamma." Certainly Alara Kalama abides knowing and seeing this Dhamma.' Then I went to Alara Kalama and asked him: 'Friend Kalama, in what way do you declare that by realizing for yourself with direct knowledge you enter upon and abide in this Dhamma?' In reply he declared the base of nothingness (*akincanna-ayatana*).

"I considered: 'Not only Alara Kalama has faith, energy, mindfulness, concentration (*samadhi*), and wisdom. I too have faith, energy, mindfulness, concentration, and wisdom. Suppose

I endeavor to realize the Dhamma that Alara Kalama declares he enters upon and abides in by realizing for himself with direct knowledge?'

"I soon quickly entered upon and abided in that Dhamma by realizing for myself with direct knowledge. Then I went to Alara Kalama and asked him: 'Friend Kalama, is it in this way that you declare that you enter upon and abide in this Dhamma by realizing for yourself with direct knowledge?' —— 'That is the way, friend.' —— 'It is in this way, friend, that I also enter upon and abide in this Dhamma by realizing for myself with direct knowledge.' —— 'It is a gain for us, friend, it is a great gain for us that we have such a venerable one for our companion in the holy life (*subrahma-carin*). So the Dhamma that I declare I enter upon and abide in by realizing for myself with direct knowledge is the Dhamma that you enter upon and abide in by realizing for yourself with direct knowledge. And the Dhamma that you enter upon and abide in by realizing for yourself with direct knowledge is the Dhamma that I declare I enter upon and abide in by realizing for myself with direct knowledge. So you know the Dhamma that I know and I know the Dhamma that you know. As I am, so are you; as your are, so am I. Come, friend, let us now lead the community together.'

"Thus Alara Kalama, my teacher, placed me, his pupil, on an equal footing with himself and awarded me the highest honor. But it occurred to me: 'This Dhamma does not lead to disenchantment, to dispassion, to cessation, to peace, to direct knowledge, to enlightenment, to Nibbana, but only to reappearance in the base of nothingness.' Not being satisfied with that Dhamma, I left it and went away."

In short, when Gotama realized that Alara Kalama's wisdom was far from nirvana he left him.

Alara is mentioned again in the sutra *The Buddha's Last Days*. Pukkusa, one of Alara's disciples, speaks of his teacher in glowing terms, praising him as an expert at tranquil abiding from long ago. The sutra tells us that Pukkusa was from Malla, so we know that Alara's fame spread at least as far as Malla, a country located near Nepal.

# The Visit to Uddaka the Ascetic

Chronicles of the Buddha's later life note that the ascetic Uddaka Ramaputta (P.; Udraka Ramaputra, Skt.) was known for his teachings on the base of neither-perception-nor-non-perception. We are told that "Ramaputta means the child of Rama." The *Lalitavistara*, a biographical account of the Buddha, gives no concrete information about the contents of Uddaka's teaching but does say he answered a question from the Buddha with the statement: "I didn't have a teacher. I attained realization naturally, by myself."

*The Noble Search* continues with an account of their meeting:

> "Still in search, bhikkhus, of what is whole-some, seeking the supreme state of sublime peace, I went to Uddaka Ramaputta and said to him: 'Friend, I want to lead the holy life in this Dhamma and Discipline.' Uddaka Ramaputta replied: 'The venerable one may stay here. This Dhamma is such that a wise man can soon enter upon and abide in it, realizing for himself through direct knowledge his own teacher's doctrine.' I soon quickly learned that Dhamma. As far as mere lip-reciting and rehearsal of his teaching went, I could speak with knowledge and assurance, and I claimed, 'I know and see'——and there were others who did likewise.
>
> "I considered: 'It is not through mere faith alone that Rama declared: "By realizing for myself with direct knowledge, I enter upon and abide in this Dhamma." Certainly Rama abided knowing and seeing this Dhamma.' Then I went to Uddaka Ramaputta and asked him: 'Friend, in what way did Rama declare that by realizing for himself with direct knowledge he entered upon and abided in this Dhamma?' In reply Uddaka Ramaputta de-clared the base of neither-perception-nor-non-perception.
>
> "I considered: 'Not only Rama had faith, energy, mindfulness, concentration, and wisdom. I

too have faith, energy, mindfulness, concentration, and wisdom. Suppose I endeavor to realize the Dhamma that Rama declared he entered upon and abided in by realizing for himself with direct knowledge?'

"I soon quickly entered upon and abided in that Dhamma by realizing for myself with direct knowledge. Then I went to Uddaka Ramaputta and asked him: 'Friend, was it in this way that Rama declared that he entered upon and abided in this Dhamma by realizing for himself with direct knowledge?' —— 'That is the way, friend.' —— 'It is in this way, friend, that I also enter upon and abide in this Dhamma by realizing for myself with direct knowledge.' —— 'It is a gain for us, friend, it is a great gain for us that we have such a venerable one for our companion in the holy life. So the Dhamma that Rama declared he entered upon and abided in by realizing for himself with direct knowledge is the Dhamma that you enter upon and abide in by realizing for yourself with direct knowledge. And the Dhamma that you enter upon and abide in by realizing for yourself with direct knowledge is the Dhamma that Rama declared he entered upon and abided in by realizing for himself with direct knowledge. So you know the Dhamma that Rama knew and Rama knew the Dhamma that you know. As Rama was, so are you; as you are, so was Rama. Come, friend, now lead this community.'

"Thus Uddaka Ramaputta, my companion in

the holy life, placed me in the position of a teacher and awarded me the highest honor. But it occurred to me: 'This Dhamma does not lead to disenchantment, to dispassion, to cessation, to peace, to direct knowledge, to enlightenment, to Nibbana, but only to reappearance in the base of neither-perception-nor-non-perception.' Not being satisfied with that Dhamma, I left it and went away."

When Gotama realized that Uddaka Ramaputta's wisdom was far from nirvana he left him as well.

# Beginning Ascetic Austerities

Gotama was so disappointed in the teaching of the two renowned sages Alara Kalama and Uddaka Ramaputta that he decided he would have to find the path to wisdom by himself.

He decided to try a regimen of ascetic austerities.

We don't know of anything similar among the Greek philosophers, any attempt to use special training in the search for wisdom itself. We can assume that these men tried to develop their powers of concentration in order to improve their speculative ability, but we have no evidence of any specific training performed for that purpose.

This would seem to be another area of difference

between how the Greeks and the Buddha went about their pursuit of wisdom.

Anyway, in his quest for wisdom Gotama began to practice what are called 'ascetic austerities'.

The chronicles of the Buddha's life and the sutras generally tell us that Shakyamuni left home at 29 and practiced austerities in the mountains and forests for a period of 6 years. As a result, his body became emaciated and his color turned a deathly gray, but he was not able to attain the highest realization. In the end he came to the conclusion that austerities were not the path to the truth and forsook them. He ate some milk porridge brought to him by a young girl of the village and bathed himself in the river. His spirits thus revived, he traveled to Bodhgaya and sat down quietly beneath a bo tree he found there and began to meditate. He finally attained realization, and thus became the Awakened One.

He describes his movements in *The Noble Search*:

"Still in search, bhikkhus, of what is wholesome, seeking the supreme state of sublime peace, I wandered by stages through the Magadhan country until eventually I arrived at Senanigama near Uruvela. There I saw an agreeable piece of ground, a delightful grove with a clear-flowing river with pleasant, smooth banks and nearby a village for alms resort. I considered: 'This is an agreeable piece of ground, this is a delightful grove with a clear-flowing river with pleasant, smooth banks and nearby a village for alms resort. This will serve for the striving of a clansman intent

on striving.' And I sat down there thinking: 'This
will serve for striving.'"

He details the course of his asceticism in *The Greater
Discourse to Saccaka*.

At first he tries to concentrate his mind with yoga-like
practice:

> "I thought: 'Suppose, with my teeth clenched
> and my tongue pressed against the roof of my
> mouth, I beat down, constrain, and crush mind
> with mind.' So, with my teeth clenched and my
> tongue pressed against the roof of my mouth, I
> beat down, constrained, and crushed mind with
> mind. While I did so, sweat ran from my armpits.
> Just as a strong man might seize a weaker man by
> the head or shoulders and beat him down, con-
> strain him, and crush him, so too, with my teeth
> clenched and my tongue pressed against the roof
> of my mouth, I beat down, constrained, and
> crushed mind with mind, and sweat ran from my
> armpits. But although tireless energy was aroused
> in me and unremitting mindfulness was estab-
> lished, my body was overwrought and uncalm
> because I was exhausted by the painful striving.
> But such painful feeling that arose in me did not
> invade my mind and remain."

Secondly, he tries methods of breath control:

"I thought: 'Suppose I practice the breathingless

meditation.' So I stopped the in-breaths and out-breaths through my mouth and nose. While I did so, there was a loud sound of winds coming out from my earholes. Just as there is a loud sound when a smith's bellows are blown, so too, while I stopped the in-breaths and out-breaths through my nose and ears, there was a loud sound of winds coming out from my earholes. But although tireless energy was aroused in me and unremitting mindfulness was established, my body was overwrought and uncalm because I was exhausted by the painful striving. But such painful feeling that arose in me did not invade my mind and remain."

"Now when deities saw me, some said: 'The recluse Gotama is dead.' Other deities said: 'The recluse Gotama is not dead, he is dying.' And other deities said: 'The recluse Gotama is not dead nor dying; he is an arahant, for such is the way arahants abide.'"

Thirdly, he tries the method of fasting:

"I thought: 'Suppose I practice entirely cutting off food.' Then deities came to me and said: 'Good sir, do not practice entirely cutting off food. If you do so, we shall infuse heavenly food into the pores of your skin and you will live on that.' I considered: 'If I claim to be completely fasting while these deities infuse heavenly food into the pores of my skin and I live on that, then I shall by lying.' So I dismissed those deities, saying: 'There is no need.'

"I thought: 'Suppose I take very little food, a handful each time, whether of bean soup or lentil soup or vetch soup or pea soup.' So I took very little food, a handful each time, whether of bean soup or lentil soup or vetch soup or pea soup. While I did so, my body reached a state of extreme emaciation."

It is written that the Buddha performed these and similar austerities for a period of six or seven years.

What kind of wisdom did he obtain as a result of his efforts?

Many of the chronicles tell us that he obtained none. One of the *Jataka Tales* says:

(The Great One) performed austerities for a period of six years but this time was spent in vain. It was like he was trying to tie knots in the thin air. He thought: "These austerities are not the path to enlightenment," and went to beg alms in the towns and villages so that he could have some solid food to eat.

When (the Great One) gave up practicing austerities and went out into the villages to beg for alms food, the five ascetics who were with him felt like he had gone astray and they deserted him.

His five companion bhikkhus said, "This person has performed austerities for six years but he has not been able to attain the wisdom of one who knows everything. Now he has gone to the villages to get alms food, but what will that accomplish? He has taken up luxurious ways and abandoned his diligent enterprise. Looking for something special from him is like trying to wash your face with a single drop of dew. We can receive no benefit from being with him," and went on their way. They took up their bowls and robes, travelled for a distance of 18 *yojana*, and entered the Deer Park (Isipatana).

In *The Greater Discourse on the Lion's Roar* an aged Gotama Buddha looks back on the past and tells his disciple Sariputta about the extreme austerities he practiced when he was younger. The Buddha describes them in detail, and then concludes that they were ultimately meaningless:

> "Yet, Sariputta, by such conduct, by such practice, by such performance of austerities, I did not attain any superhuman states, any distinction in knowledge and vision worthy of the noble ones. Why was that? Because I did not attain that noble wisdom which when attained is noble and emancipating and leads the one who practices in accordance with it to the complete destruction of suffering."

In *The Greater Discourse to Saccaka* the Buddha speaks about giving up the practice of austerities in concrete terms. After describing his disappointment in the teachings of Alara Kalama and Uddaka the son of Rama, he explains how he practiced solitary austerities by himself and then ends by saying:

> "I considered: 'It is not easy to attain that pleasure with a body so excessively emaciated. Suppose I ate some solid food——some boiled rice and bread.' And I ate some solid food——some boiled rice and bread. Now at that time five bhikkhus were waiting upon me, thinking: 'If our recluse Gotama achieves some higher state, he will inform us.' But when I ate the boiled rice and bread, the five bhikkhus were disgusted and left me, thinking: 'The recluse Gotama now lives luxuriously; he has given up his striving and reverted to luxury.'
>
> "Now when I had eaten solid food and regained my strength, then quite secluded from sensual pleasures, secluded from unwholesome states, I entered upon and abided in the first jhana, which is accompanied by applied and sustained thought, with rapture and pleasure born of seclusion."

The Buddha continues to describe how he entered and abided in the four jhanas, one after another.

# The Contents of the Buddha's Enlightenment

When the Buddha finally realized that austerities were useless he abandoned their practice, ate some milk porridge, regained his strength and energy, sat under the *ashvattha* tree (bodhi tree) in meditation, and, then, at last, attained supreme enlightenment.

What was the nature of this enlightenment? What kind of wisdom did the Buddha realize?

The Buddha's wisdom consisted of the realization of Four Truths and the Twelve-Linked Chain of Dependent Origination.

The Twelve-Linked Chain of Dependent Origination is a chain of interrelated phenomena, the examination of which reveals the exact manner in which human suffering and affliction arise. It is composed of twelve divisions, or links, that are seen to form a series. These are:

| | |
|---|---|
| Ignorance (*avijja*) | Ignorance |
| Actions (*sankhara*) | The subliminal power of formation, the faculty of activity |
| Consciousness (*vinnana*) | The faculty of cognition |
| Name and Form (*nama-rupa*) | Name and form, or mind and matter, mind and body |

| | |
|---|---|
| The Six Sense Organs (*salayatana*) | The six places that establish the faculty of the mind: eyes, ears, nose, tongue, body, mind |
| Contact (*phassa*) | Contact between the six organs of sensory awareness and their objects |
| Feeling (*vedana*) | The faculty of feeling |
| Craving (*tanha*) | Blind instinct, delusion, likened to the desire to quench thirst |
| Grasping (*upadana*) | Attachment |
| Becoming (*bhava*) | Being |
| Birth (*jati*) | To be born |
| Old Age and Death (*jara-marana*) | The form of impermanence |

We have here an ordered sequence of conditions in which the former element establishes the latter. Or, in reverse, it is a sequence in which the extinction of the former element brings about the extinction of the latter.

The *Vinaya Pitaka* says:

At the time the World-Honored One abided at the foot of the bodhi tree on the banks of the Neranjara River.

He attained Enlightenment for the first time.

Then he remained seated in meditation posture for seven days and took joy in his liberation.

When the seven days had passed, he came out of his meditation and in the first watch of the night began a deep contemplation of the forward exposition of the law of dependent origination.

He considered: When this exists, that exists; with the arising of this, that arises.

On ignorance depend actions. On actions depend consciousness. On consciousness depend name and form. On name and form depend the six sense organs. On the six sense organs depends contact. On contact depends feeling. On feeling depends craving. On craving depends grasping. On grasping depends becoming. On becoming depends birth. On birth depend old age and death, grief, sorrow, suffering, lamentation, and worry. Thus does the whole aggregation of suffering arise.

The Buddha then contemplated the reversal of the sequence:

(Abandon clinging and) with the remainderless fading away and cessation of ignorance, actions cease; with the cessation of actions, consciousness ceases; with the cessation of consciousness, name and form cease; with the cessation of name and form, the six sense organs cease; with the cessation of the six sense organs, contact ceases; with the cessation of contact, feeling ceases; with the cessation of feeling, craving ceases; with the cessation of craving, grasping ceases; with the cessation of grasping, becoming ceases; with the cessation of becoming, birth ceases; with the cessation of birth, old age and death, grief, sorrow, suffering, lamentation, and worry cease. Thus does the whole aggregation of suffering cease.

Then the World-Honored One, having realized the significance of this truth, recites a poem of jubilation:

If these Dhammas were to become known
To the Brahmin who is striving
His doubts would entirely cease
Because he would understand cause
(and its relationship to effect as clearly delineated
in the doctrine of dependent origination).

# The Law of Dependent Origination

The doctrine that the Buddha realized beneath the bodhi tree was the Law of Dependent Origination. It consists of two facets: the Twelve-Linked Chain of Dependent Origination, listed above, and the Four Sacred Truths.

The Pali term for dependent origination is *paticca-samuppada*, a combination of the word *paticca* meaning condition and the word *samuppada* meaning arising. Any arising is the result of a condition.

Dependent origination means that phenomena occur through conditions; that all phenomena come into being through their dependency on conditions and all phenomena are extinguished through their dependency on conditions. The Buddha's doctrine of dependent origination teaches that nothing exists which does not change. All phenomena arise as a result of conditions, all phenomena change as a result of conditions, and all phenomena cease as a result of conditions. This doctrine led to a succession of fundamental concepts, such as 'the non-self of the five aggregates', 'the devoid nature of self', and 'emptiness'.

The four sacred truths are a clear and direct expression of the true nature of the arising and cessation of all phenomena. They are based on a theoretical formula:

> When this exists, that comes to be,
> > with the arising of this, that arises.
> When this does not exist, that does not come to be,
> > with the cessation of this, that ceases.

The Buddha applies this formula to the suffering of the human condition and arrives at the Four Noble Truths.

He declares this doctrine throughout the Agama[2] Sutras. This early rendering is found in sutra 56.31 of the

---

[2]The Agama Sutras are a classification of early Buddhist scripture written in Sanskrit. The Chinese canon, which was originally translated from these Sanskrit scriptures, is therefore also referred to as the Agamas. The Pali canon, which differs somewhat from the Sanskrit, is generally called the Nikaya Sutras. Sometimes, however, it is referred to as the Agama Sutras as well.

*Samyutta Nikaya* of the Pali Canon and sutra 15.45 of the *Samyukta Agama* of the Chinese Canon.

1  This is suffering
   *Idam dukkham*
2  This is the arising of suffering
   *Ayam dukkhasamudayo*
3  This is the ceasing of suffering
   *Ayam dukkhanirodho*
4  This is the practice that leads to the ceasing of suffering
   *Ayam dukkhanirodhagamini patipada*

Sometimes the sutras state the Four Noble Truths like this:

> Bhikkhus, this is the noble truth of suffering.
> Bhikkhus, this is the noble truth of the cause of suffering.
> Bhikkhus, this is the noble truth of the termination of suffering.
> Bhikkhus, this is the noble truth of the way to the termination of suffering.

The Chinese abbreviated this formulation to:
   Truth of Suffering
   Truth of Aggregation
   Truth of Cessation
   Truth of the Path

And, finally, we can summarize:

Suffering
Aggregation
Cessation
Path

This is the dharma of the Four Noble Truths.

Along with the Twelve-Linked Chain of Dependent Origination, it is part of the content of the legendary enlightenment that the Buddha experienced under the bodhi tree.

Do these two doctrines represent the ultimate wisdom of the Buddha, what he calls nirvana?

# The Two Phases of the Buddha's Path to Wisdom

I'd like here to advance my own views on this subject.

The majority of Buddhist chronicles and sutras claim that the Buddha's 6 years of austerities were useless.

The Buddha is said to have voiced this opinion himself.

Could this be true?

I don't think so.

Just think about it. Here we have this tremendous genius who spent 6 years totally absorbed in contemplation while performing a death-defying regimen of ascetic practices.

Can we really believe that all that effort bore no fruit? We already know that the Buddha visited Alara

Kalama and Uddaka Ramaputta, two of the most highly realized sages of his day, to receive instruction. He managed to attain the realization of the essence of their teachings, the base of nothingness and the base of neither-perception-nor-non-perception, in a relatively short period of time. He had such a good mind that both of these sages invited the Buddha to become a preceptor to their own disciples.

So I don't believe we should take the assertions that the Buddha was wasting his time literally.

Instead, I believe that the course of spiritual practice that led the Buddha to the attainment of wisdom can be divided into two separate phases.

The first of these is the six-year period of austerities.

The second is the period of tranquil abiding that he spent under the bodhi tree after he stopped practicing austerities and ate solid food.

Furthermore, I have come to think that the Buddha actually attained the complete realization of the Twelve-Linked Chain of Dependent Origination and the Four Noble Truths during the first phase of his practice, the austerity period.

I also believe that the Twelve-Linked Chain of Dependent Origination and the Four Noble Truths are not the ultimate wisdom that the Buddha sought. They are not nirvana. These concepts do represent a given level of wisdom on the way to nirvana, certainly, but this level is still a long way from the supreme wisdom of nirvana. I suspect that the Buddha, given his brilliance, probably attained this level of understanding in one or two, at the most three, years after beginning his course of spiritual discipline.

In passing, I can also imagine that, with their brains, Socrates, Plato, or Aristotle would have attained similar levels of realization in two or three years if they had focused their contemplation in a similar direction.

The Buddha continued practicing austerities for 6 years, even after he realized Dependent Origination and the Noble Truths, because he knew that this wisdom was still far from the wisdom of nirvana. He continued spiritual practice because he had not yet found the supreme wisdom he was seeking.

Then, sometime after he entered his sixth year of discipline, it dawned on him that further progress on his present path was impossible. Something clicked inside of him. He felt a surge of excitement when he intuited that there was another way to make the leap into new, higher levels of wisdom.

He gave up his position of the last 6 years and decisively left it behind.

This is when he went to meditate under the bodhi tree where he finally attained the wisdom of nirvana.

And what sort of wisdom did this turn out to be?

# Plato and Nirvana

As I mentioned earlier, the Buddha doesn't really tell us anything about it.

He simply instructs:

'You should first realize Nirvāṇa and then you can know what it is. You need not know that even. The attainment of Nirvāṇa will give you freedom from births and rebirths, which means emancipation.'

The Buddha leaves us dangling about the true meaning of the word.

Here is what I have been able to surmise.

First, remember these comments I made in the section on 'The Practice of Death':

There is a famous quote from Plato that says philosophy is the 'practice of death' (*meditatio mortis*).

Briefly, he says that insofar as we are restricted by the conditions of life here on earth, we are unable to attain the wisdom that is the fundamental goal of philosophy. We can only attain wisdom through the pure selfhood that is obtained when we are released completely from these limitations.

Having come this far in our discussion, we begin to see an element that is important in our comparison of the wisdom of Greek philosophy and the wisdom of Gotama Buddha. Dr. Tozu focuses on it in the following passage.

I then go on to quote Dr. Tozu.

The passage contains the opinions of both Plato and

Dr. Tozu, and, I would suggest, it sounds like they are referring to nirvana:

> We should note here that all the bonds that restrict the soul are somehow related to the physical body. So the only way for the soul to be completely free to attain its own selfhood is to find release from the physical body. And this, of course, means death. Hence death becomes a requirement for the purity of soul necessary to perceive true wisdom. From here, Plato maintains, the soul is able to enter its original, or eternal, life.
>
> Plato is not conjuring some vague paean to death the way one might glorify life. Rather, he is saying that the ultimate state to which philosophy aspires must be that of death. This raises a very interesting problem, for, if the ultimate goal of philosophy turns out to be death, it would seem that the question of philosophy's utility for this life becomes meaningless.

Plato's thinking reaches its consummation with this idea that the physical body must be extinguished in order for the self to obtain pure wisdom. Platonic philosophy contends that one can enter the realm of liberation from physical bondage and attain the true wisdom born from the purity of the discrete soul only after one has 'died'.

Indeed, is this not nirvana?

How appropriate. It would seem that what Plato (and Socrates) was aspiring towards is nirvana. Nirvana is what they were looking for.

Unfortunately, however, Plato says one can only get there through death, whereas the Buddha was able to reach nirvana while still alive, after his practice of spiritual austerities.

Still and all, the Buddha did have to undergo 6 years of mortally extreme austerities, where, in a sense, he had to "abandon the body and become pure self," or, in Platonic terms, "become pure soul alone." These 6 years were absolutely necessary. They were definitely not a waste of time.

Entering nirvana while still alive, as the Buddha did, is known as 'nirvana with a remainder'. This term means one who has entered nirvana but possesses a physical body.

# The Practices of Wisdom that Lead to Nirvana

Does this mean that we have to look to the writings of the Greek philosophers to understand the meaning of nirvana?

No, of course not.

A careful examination of the Agamas and the Nikayas, the collections of sutras containing scriptures that the Buddha taught, reveals texts that seem to reflect the meaning of nirvana.

We also find sutras that contain methods of spiritual practice which teach us how to attain the wisdom of nirvana for ourselves.

This complete methodology has been named 'the 7 systems and 37 elements of enlightenment' or 'the 37 practices for attaining nirvana'. Since it consists of 7 topics and 37 subjects to be learned, I call it 'the 7 systems and 37 curricula for the attainment of sacred wisdom'.

Many people who focus on Mahayana doctrine are not aware that these practices exist as part of the Buddhist canon. This is a truly unfortunate situation, for these are the very practices that can turn an ordinary person into a genius.

This following description of these practices is taken from the *Kinti Sutta*, sutra 103 of the *Majjhima Nikaya* of the Pali Canon. The Buddha says:

> "So, bhikkhus, these things that I have taught you after directly knowing them — that is, the Four Foundations of Mindfulness, the Four Right Kinds of Striving, the Four Bases for Spiritual Power, the Five Faculties, the Five Powers, the Seven Enlightenment Factors, the Noble Eightfold Path — in these things you should all train in concord, with mutual appreciation, without disputing."

Here the Buddha gives us a straight-forward list of the actual methods that he practiced in order to obtain wisdom. Further, he advises all his practitioners to practice together harmoniously, in a spirit of good will, and not to fight with one another. His instructions could not be any clearer.

Abhidharma Buddhists organized the 7 groupings of

spiritual practices found in the Agama Sutras and named them 'the 7 systems and 37 elements of enlightenment' or 'the 37 practices for attaining nirvana'. These are what bring the practitioner to enlightenment.

Here is a brief explanation of what they are:

## THE FOUR FOUNDATIONS OF MINDFULNESS

An older translation of this is the Four Stations of Mindfulness, or, similarly, the Contemplation of the Four Stations of Mindfulness.

These are four kinds of contemplation, four meditation techniques conducive to enlightenment. They are the **foundation of mindfulness of the body,** the **foundation of mindfulness of the feelings,** the **foundation of mindfulness of the mind,** and the **foundation of mindfulness of phenomena.**

In practice, one contemplates and meditates that:

1. the body is impure
2. feelings are suffering
3. the mind is impermanent
4. phenomena are devoid of self

We contemplate and meditate that our body is impure. We contemplate and meditate that all our feelings are suffering. We contemplate and meditate that our minds are impermanent. We contemplate and meditate that all phenomena are devoid of self.

In the beginning we contemplate each of these four provisions individually. Then we proceed to unify the four into one concept, contemplating and meditating that the body, feelings, mind, and all phenomena (dharma) are impure. Then that they are suffering, then that they are impermanent, then that they are devoid of self. (I believe that these are the Four Noble Truths put into practice. At the very least, there is a profound relationship between them.)

## THE FOUR RIGHT KINDS OF STRIVING

An older translation of this term is the Four Right Efforts. They are the four practices of **striving to eradicate evil, striving to produce good, striving to augment good,** and **striving to prevent evil.**

The practice of **striving to eradicate evil** =

trying to eliminate the evil that has already arisen. This elimination must be repeated many times.

The practice of **striving to produce good** =

trying to produce good that has not yet arisen

The practice of **striving to augment good** =

trying to increase and improve the good that has already arisen

The practice of **striving to prevent evil** =

trying to prevent the evil that has not yet occurred from arising

## THE FOUR BASES OF SPIRITUAL POWER

Also translated as the Four Bases of Transcendental Knowledge.

These are the foundations for the endowment of four kinds of unobstructed powers. They are four types of practice methods that produce supernatural, divine powers.

The **base of the power of the concentration of will** =
> a practice that perfects the fundamental condition of the life force, particularly as it relates to the physical body

The **base of the power of the concentration of effort** =
> a practice that leads to a dramatic improvement in the basic condition of the physical body, rooted in the accomplishment of the previous power

The **base of the power of the concentration of mind** =
> a practice that leads to a strengthening of mental abilities based on the improvement in the physical abilities. This development occurs gradually, jumping from stage to stage. This base initiates, by human agency, evolutionary developments in the old cortex (archi-cortex) which set the stage for later reinforcement of the deficient areas of the brain.

The **base of the power of the concentration of investigation** =
> a practice that induces development in the new brain, or neocortex. It also opens up the interbrain, the locus of spirituality. This brings about the complete unification of intelligence and spirituality in the practitioner.

## THE FIVE FACULTIES

The Five Faculties, or Five Roots, are the **root of faith,** the **root of striving,** the **root of mindfulness,** the **root of concentration,** and the **root of wisdom.**

Faculty (root) means an ability that you have free use of. The practices that produce the supreme abilities that lead to nirvana are faith in the three jewels of the Buddha, dharma, and sangha, constant effort, mindfulness, concentration (meditation), and wisdom.

## THE FIVE POWERS

The Five Powers are the **power of faith,** the **power of striving,** the **power of mindfulness,** the **power of concentration,** and the **power of wisdom** (or the power of knowledge).

These are the practices that endow us with the five higher powers to achieve nirvana.

The Five Powers have the same virtuous subjects as the Five Roots. The roots deal with ability, whereas these represent a more advanced level of power. They can be viewed, therefore, as differing in degree but not in kind.

## THE SEVEN ENLIGHTENMENT FACTORS

The Seven Factors are the **factor of discrimination of the dharma,** the **factor of striving,** the **factor of joy,** the **factor of tranquillity,** the **factor of detachment,** the **factor of concentration,** and the **factor of mindfulness.**

These are seven practices that lead to nirvana.

The **factor of discrimination of the dharma** =
the practice of the discernment of distinguishing the true doctrine from false doctrine

The **factor of striving** =
the practice of diligently maintaining one's concentrated effort with no backsliding

The **factor of joy** =
the practice of rejoicing in the study and application of

the true dharma

The **factor of tranquillity** =

the practice of eliminating fogginess and sluggishness and attaining a state of clarity and relaxation in one's body and mind

The **factor of detachment** =

the practice of achieving balance and securing serenity of mind by divorcing it from discrimination, hatred, and attachment. It is the practice of detaching one's thoughts from external objects.

The **factor of concentration** =

the practice of attaining a concentrated mind during both the activities of meditation and those of daily life

The **factor of mindfulness** =

the practice of maintaining equilibrium

## THE NOBLE EIGHTFOLD PATH (THE RIGHT EIGHTFOLD PATH)

These are the eight practices that lead to the realm of the ideal.

**Right view** =

correct meditation on the dharma principle of the Four Noble Truths

**Right thought** =

correct contemplation on the dharma principle of the Four Noble Truths

**Right speech** =

to speak correctly

**Right action** =

to live correctly

**Right livelihood** =

to perform correct actions of body, speech, and mind
to live in accordance with correct principles

**Right effort** =
to strive correctly for attainment

**Right mindfulness** =
to be continually concentrated and aware of the correct path, never falling into a scattered state of inattention

**Right concentration** =
to enter into the realm of pure, firm enlightenment

In other words, the eight practices of the Noble Path are correct view, correct thoughts, correct words, correct actions, correct lifestyle, correct efforts, correct attention, and correct mental concentration.

These, then, are 'the 7 systems and 37 practices for attaining nirvana'.

The Four Foundations of Mindfulness and the Five Faculties (Roots of Emancipation) are forms of meditation.

The Four Right Efforts, the Five Powers, the Seven Enlightenment Factors, and the Noble Eightfold Path are forms of meditation and practice.

The Four Bases of Spiritual Power are forms of *tapas* (intensive spiritual exercises). 'Spiritual' here means divine, or supernatural, and thus the Four Bases of Spiritual Power are four kinds of spiritual practices that generate divine, supernatural abilities.

When you were reading this explanation, did you notice anything unusual?

One of the 7 systems seems to be of a somewhat

different nature than the others.

*The four bases of spiritual power*

This doesn't sound like an expression that the Buddha, in his theoretical teaching of the dharma, would use.

Here is an excerpt from a sutra that discusses the Four Bases of Spiritual Power. It contains expressions that seem even more unlikely.

# Visions of Nirvana

The following excerpts are taken from sutras 51. 11 of the *Samyutta Nikaya*:

"(When he accomplishes the Four Bases of Spiritual Power), a bhikkhu wields the various kinds of supernormal power: having been one, he becomes many; having been many he becomes one; he appears and vanishes; he goes unhindered through a wall, through an enclosure, through a mountain, as though through space; he dives in and out of the earth as though it were water; he walks on water without sinking as though it were earth; seated cross-legged, he travels in space like a bird; with his hand he touches and strokes the moon and sun so powerful and mighty; he wields bodily mastery even as far as the Brahma-world.

"(When he accomplishes the Four Bases of Spiritual Power), a bhikkhu, with the divine ear element, which is purified and surpasses the human, he hears both kinds of sounds, the divine and the human, those that are far as well as near.

"(When he accomplishes the Four Bases of Spiritual Power), a bhikkhu understands the minds of other beings, of other persons, having encompassed them with his own mind. He understands a mind affected by lust as affected by lust and a mind unaffected by lust as unaffected by lust; he understands a mind affected by hate as affected by hate and a mind unaffected by hate as unaffected by hate; he understands a mind affected by delusion as affected by delusion and a mind unaffected by delusion as unaffected by delusion; he understands a contracted mind as contracted and a distracted mind as distracted; he understands an exalted mind as exalted and an unexalted mind as unexalted; he understands a surpassed mind as surpassed and an unsurpassed mind as unsurpassed; he understands a concentrated mind as concentrated and an unconcentrated mind as unconcentrated; he understands a liberated mind as liberated and an unliberated mind as unliberated.

"(When he accomplishes the Four Bases of Spiritual Power), a bhikkhu recollects his manifold past lives, that is, one birth, two births, three births, four births, five births, ten births, twenty births, thirty births, forty births, fifty births, a hundred births, a thousand births, a hundred thousand births, many aeons of world-contraction and expansion: 'There I was so named, of such a clan (*gotta*), with such a caste (*vanna*), such was my nutriment, such my experience of pleasure and pain, such my life-term; and passing away from there, I reappeared here.' Thus with their aspects and particulars he recollects his manifold past lives.

"(When he accomplishes the Four Bases of Spiritual Power), a bhikkhu directs (his mind) to knowledge of the passing away and reappearance of beings. With the divine eye, which is purified and surpasses the human, he sees beings passing away and reappearing, inferior and superior, fair and ugly, fortunate and unfortunate. He understands how beings pass on according to their actions thus: 'These worthy beings who were ill-conducted in body, speech, and mind, revilers of noble ones, wrong in their views, giving effet to wrong view in their actions, on the dissolution of the body, after death, have reappeared in a state of deprivation, in a bad destination, in perdition, even in hell; but these worthy beings who were well-conducted in body, speech, and mind, not revilers of noble ones, right in their views, giving effect to right view in their actions, on the dissolution of the body, after death, have reappeared in a good destination, even in the heavenly world.' Thus with the divine eye, which is purified and surpasses the human, he sees beings passing away and reappearing, inferior and superior, fair and ugly, fortunate and unfortunate, and he understands how beings pass on according to their actions."

The passage concludes:

"(When he accomplishes the Four Bases of Spiritual Power), by realizing for himself with direct knowledge, he here and now enters upon and abides in the deliverance of mind and deliverance by wisdom that are taintless with the destruction of the taints."

Ultimately, then, the Buddha attained liberation through the practice of the Four Bases of Spiritual Power. Performing the intensive discipline of these four bases is how the Buddha finally reached nirvana.

This passage contains expressions that differ from the Buddha's usual style of oratory, which tends to be more composed and logical. To wit:

*...seated cross-legged, he travels in space like a bird; with his hand he touches and strokes the moon and sun so powerful and mighty...*

I mean, what is he actually saying?

Do you know what I think? I think this whole passage describes the Buddha's visions of nirvana.

In fact, I think we may have found the Buddha's statement of what nirvana is really like.

I also think it's clear there is no way he could have described nirvana without resorting to such unusual expressions.

And this is why he always counseled:

"First experience nirvana for yourself.

Then you will understand what it is."

...Intellectual knowledge about the nature of nirvana is beside the point. It doesn't matter what I say because words won't help you understand it....

# Creating Appropriate Systems for the Age of Wisdom

I recently accepted an invitation to attend a symposium, Forum 1999, which was sponsored by the Dentsu Corporation.

The invitation listed three prestigious presenters: Paul Krugman from MIT, Heizo Takenaka from Keio University, and Glen Fukushima. The theme of the forum was "The Search for Breakthroughs in Knowledge" and the title of the panel discussion was 'Strategies for Surviving the Global Competition in Intelligence'. I was attracted by the line-up of speakers, but even more so by the subject matter, and made time in my busy schedule to participate. I was very pleased that I did so because all three of the lectures were excellent.

I was particularly impressed with Dr. Takenaka's presentation, and quote from it here:

> ...As we face the 21st century, we see the emergence into the world of a new kind of marketplace, one that undoubtedly reflects the revolution in the telecommunications industry. We are entering into an age of wisdom. We must

reform our social systems to conform to this new age. Today I refer to this as 'soft power reform'.

It is imperative that governments institute economic policies as though they were in a state of rational emergency. Next, we need structural reforms to keep us competitive in the changing global marketplace.

Further, we need to create the kind of social systems that are suited to this age of wisdom.

We must actualize these objectives.

Truth be told, I had just started writing this book when I attended the forum and had already decided to use the words *The Age of Wisdom* in the title. So I was quite excited to hear these very words escape the lips of Dr. Takenaka. I felt like he had been reading my mind and gotten the point of what I was trying to say.

*Creating the kind of social systems that are suited to this age of wisdom.*

That's it exactly. Any country, business, or individual that doesn't do this will only collapse and fall out of the race.

So how can we accomplish it?

*Creating the kind of social systems that are suited to this age of wisdom.*

He's right, but what can we do to make it happen?

Isn't the first thing we have to do produce people who have the wisdom to make these systems possible?

Before we create social systems of wisdom don't we have to create systems that produce people who have wisdom?

Does any system like that already exist?

The world contains a vast number of educational institutions. But education and wisdom are two different things. We see a surfeit of educated fools. Wisdom, as Socrates says, is not a commodity that can be handed off from one person to another. Wisdom is something that you have to find within yourself.

# Cultivating Wisdom by Direct Mental Training

In this regard, George Gallup of the Gallup Research Institute has the following to say. He is of the opinion that American education does almost nothing to develop human intelligence:

"[No] system of public education [is] notably successful in giving a substantial number of students a mastery of the major fields of knowledge or the essential communication skills. These are serious shortcomings. By far the most important defect is the failure to develop to any great extent the intellectual capacities of students. Amazingly little effort is made by the educational systems of Western nations to set the mind of the student in motion——to provide him with the kind of education that will enable him to cope with new situations as they arise, help him to sharpen his critical judgement, develop more fully his creative talents, and show him how to go about producing new and better solutions to his own and society's problems ... It will always be important for students to know the great ideas, the great works, and the great events of the history of man. Nevertheless, this is not the only or even the primary objective. It is equally certain that the training of the mind itself must assume prime importance...

"Strong support for the proposal to train mental functions comes from Aldous Huxley. He says the time has come to think of training directly the mind 'that has to do the learning and the living'." (Gallup, 1964: pp. 46–47)

Gallup specifically cites concentration as one method of directly training the mind:

"The statement has been made that, broadly speaking, mental powers are effective in proportion to the degree of concentration with which they are employed. In view of the fact that men make use of only a small part of their mental capacities, importance must be attached to the ability to make more efficient use of the mental functions that are brought into play.

"Concentration is certainly one of the talents.

"The ability to concentrate can obviously be trained. In the pursuit of religious goals, many cults in India have known for centuries how to develop, through exercises patiently and persistently followed, the ability to concentrate the mind to an extraordinary degree. There is nothing secret about their training; countless books have been written on the subject.

"Undoubtedly, the reason why more attention has not been paid to such methods is that the ends and the means become so confused that the training of concentration through exercises earnestly pursued takes on the coloration of a religious observance. Because control of the mind is associated with cults, it is often looked upon as an occult art, tied up with mystical religious rites, rather than as a practical necessity in the world of today and tomorrow." (Gallup, 1964: pp. 51–52)

I completely agree with him.

George Gallup may be speaking about the Western educational system, but this statement could be applied to education in any country in the world. Contemporary educational systems do not have the methods and techniques to increase intellectual capacity directly. They can only do this indirectly.

Contemporary education tries to raise intelligence levels by using teaching methods that rely on rote memorization. It seems they imagine they can achieve two objectives for their students at one and the same time: the memorization of facts and the increase of intellectual capacity. But there is a crucial flaw in this system. This approach will not work for those students who have less memory capacity. And herein lies the critical contradiction.

The attempt to improve intellectual capacity through enforced memorization is ineffective for those who have difficulty in memorizing things to begin with.

To accept the limits that such people start out with as though they cannot be helped is out of the question. However, I am not dismissing contemporary educational methods out of hand. The educational approach of increasing intellectual capacity, while learning, has value. In itself, this should be its functional role.

What I am saying, though, is that there has to be a way of raising intellectual capacity more fundamentally, by going directly to the wellspring——the source of intelligence itself. By following this method we can increase our mental capacity. And by using this increased capacity, we can acquire higher intelligence, which in turn can then be further improved by techniques to develop mental capacity to a much greater degree.

There is a pattern of repetition here, whereby one development leads to another development that in turn carries you forward to a further development, and so on.

This is what Aldous Huxley means when he talks about the "direct training of the mind that has to do the learning and the living."

In other words, I am speaking of a technique that improves one's ability to learn by first improving the mind or that directly improves the mind while one is learning—— not a method that uses learning itself as an indirect way to improve the mind.

Wouldn't it be wonderful to have a technique that does this?

I believe that the spiritual practice of the 7 systems and 37 elements of enlightenment as found in the Agama Sutras is this very technique.

Aptly, George Gallup notes:

"Undoubtedly, the reason why more attention has not been paid to such methods is that ends and means become so confused that the training of concentration through exercise earnestly pursued takes on the coloration of a religious observance. Because control of the mind is associated with cults, it is often looked upon as an occult art, tied up with mystical religious rites, rather than as a practical necessity in the world of today and tomorrow." (Gallup, 1964: p. 52)

He's so right.

Agon Buddhism is devoted to the preservation of the teaching and methodology of the Buddha, and, as such, naturally honors the traditions of Buddhism. As George Gallup says, it has "the coloration of religious observance." But its main body of practice is the 7 systems and 37 elements that the Buddha taught in their entirety. These practices serve to cultivate wisdom through the direct training of the mind and to perfect the personality.

# Training Center

Agon-shu's commitment to mental and spiritual training is represented by the state-of-the-art practice center that we recently constructed in Kyoto.

The center is located within the precincts of our main temple in Higashiyama on a 6.8 acre parcel of land. It is a three-story building that covers an area of 35,500 square feet.

The center is equipped with special faculties like a waterfall and a fire ceremony chamber. These are available to the practitioner when he or she is ready to begin the practice of waterfall asceticism or the fire ritual (*goma*).

# The Five Steps to Nirvana

The goal of spiritual practice in Agon Buddhism is to attain nirvana.

As we all know, Gotama Buddha's ultimate teaching is that the human being can realize nirvana. Accordingly, as Buddhists, faithful disciples of the Buddha, we perform spiritual practice for the purpose of reaching that state.

Gotama Buddha showed us the way to achieve this goal by giving us his 'method for attaining Buddhahood' known as the 7 systems and 37 practices which are recorded in the Agama Sutras.

Practicing this method generates higher wisdom. It causes a graduated increase in intelligence, and, in this sense, is a method 'for improving the mind'.

Therefore, we could say that the Buddha's method is a system for creating wise men, or sages, though we shouldn't forget that the goal of the method is always nirvana.

The method progresses through five stages. They are:

1. Basic Training
2. *Srotapanna*
3. *Sakrdagamin*
4. *Anagamin*
5. *Arhat*

To explain,

a *srotapanna*——a sage who has destroyed and purified all the taints

a *sakrdagamin*——a sage who has been elevated

an *anagamin*——a sage who leaps (dimensions)

an *arhat*——a sage who has accomplished the attainment of nirvana

An *arhat* is also called a buddha.

1. Basic Training

We must prepare the body and mind so that they can endure the rigors of the spiritual practices that lead to sagehood. In a word, we have to get rid of our negative aspects, both psychological and physical.

People today have a lot of deficiencies. These need to be corrected.

The first thing we have to do is to heal the mind and

body completely.

Contemporary men and women all have a certain amount of psychological conflict and trauma stored away in the back of their minds. This trauma lurks in the layers of the human unconscious, and emerges when least expected to cause unthinkably errant and neurotic behavior. No matter how smart a person is when these conflicts emerge, he or she will not be able to function as a sound human being. In fact, the more intelligent a person is the more he or she tends to suffer from this tendency. We have to identify these problems through in-depth counseling and eliminate them. This requires analysis of both the person's subconscious and unconscious minds.

In addition to the psychological work, the practitioner needs to get adequate nutrition, sleep, and rest.

I have a theory that most people today are not eating a balanced diet. They are not getting the correct proportions of protein, fats, carbohydrates, vitamins and minerals. We don't need rich diets. We need proper ones.

Another problem we see nowadays is a tendency to insomnia, a lack of rest. We have to learn ways to relax more and sleep deeply so that we can get the rest that we need in a moderate amount of time.

We need relaxation and concentration.

If spiritual practice isn't enjoyable, people won't continue to do it. If it is just a perpetual struggle the practitioner will become dispirited and quit.

So we need to show the joy of practice.

Spiritual practice is a happy thing. One is rediscovering oneself in a whole new world. It's a real reaffirmation of self.

Not only that, but spiritual practice is enormously attractive because it enhances one's natural abilities and brings about vivid self-awakening. It has the allure of self-transformation.

While the practitioner is still in the stage of basic training, we begin to design a program of spiritual practice that is tailor-made to suit his or her needs.

There is tremendous variation in people's aptitude, personality, and stamina. And so if there are a hundred practitioners we need a hundred different practice programs.

I neglected to mention that we require a doctor's check-up at the time one begins basic training.

Let's move on to the next stage of practice.


2. *Srotapanna*——a sage who has been purified.

The practitioner is mentally, physically, and spiritually purified.

Spiritual purification often involves one's family ancestors. If any one of your ancestors led a terribly unhappy life you may experience the phenomenon known as 'repetition of fate' in which you will lead an unhappy life. This dynamic has to be resolved.

People are not born by themselves alone. You come through your parents, and inherit many things from your ancestors, whether you want them or not. In other words, there is no way that your life can ignore that of your ancestors. They have largely determined your fate.

Dr. Lipot Szondi, the world renowned psychologist who followed in the footsteps of Freud and Jung to establish the branch of psychology known as 'fate analysis'

(*Schicksalsanalyse*) or 'family depth psychology', says that the familial unconscious functions such that *"the drives of specific ancestors that are repressed in the intermediate layer of the unconscious determine the object choices a person makes in love, friendship, profession, sickness, and possibly even the mode of death."* This is what is meant by the term 'repetition of fate'.

The repressed consciousness of an ancestor who lived an unhappy, miserable existence can impel his or her descendant to lead the same kind of life. If we detect this phenomenon——Szondi's 'repetition of fate' and the offending ancestor——we have to resolve the repression.

The compulsive choices that result from the presence of the repressed consciousness of the ancestor will interfere with the success of the spiritual practice.

(For more detail on this subject please refer to my book *Channeru o Mawase* [Change the Channel].)

A *srotapanna* sage is also known as a 'stream enterer' and a 'stream opposer'.

'Stream enterer' means that he or she has newly entered the stream of sanctification.

'Stream opposer' means that he or she is moving against the currents of birth and death and karma. An ordinary person cannot help living life according to the dictates of fate, of going along with the flow of life and death and karma. He or she can't go against the tide. A *srotapanna* is able to move against the flow.

This means that this type of sage has effectively transcended the laws of birth and death and karma.

By mentally gaining control over defilements and delusion, by physically overcoming physical weakness and ill health, and by spiritually liberating oneself from the negative influences of the ancestors one is able to change the destiny, or the karma, one was born with.

3. *Sakrdagamin*——a sage who has been elevated.

A practitioner who has become a purified *srotapanna* begins the practices that elevate his or her wisdom and virtue to that of a *sakrdagamin*.

What becomes elevated?

Power and wisdom and virtue become elevated. One obtains the power and virtue and wisdom of an accomplished sage.

Parenthetically, the use of the word wisdom here is not like the wisdom of a mister know-it-all, but is the embodiment of the principles and truth that inform life itself.

According to Hajime Nakamura, Buddhism uses many different words to mean wisdom. The original Sanskrit word is *prajna* (*panna*, Pali) in which the prefix *pra* has been added to *jna* (to know). *Jna* has the same linguistic root as the Greek *gnosis* and the English 'know'.

In Chinese and Japanese, the Buddhist term for wisdom is translated into a word that is composed of two characters, one meaning resolution and the other discrimination and understanding. In Japanese it is pronounced *chie*. This word is also defined as 'the action of separating from discrimination and delusion'. As the *Ta-ch'eng-I-chang* explains in fascicle 9, the character *chi* is assigned because it means illuminating view and the character *e* is assigned because it means completed understanding.

This brief sampling shows us that the word wisdom covers a wide expanse of meaning, and that it has different grades and varieties.

The highest level of wisdom is unimaginable to anyone who doesn't actually possess it.

I imagine that the wisdom of the real sage is that sort of wisdom.

Virtue is power. Real power is something that comes from virtue. Real power elevates oneself, elevates other people, and elevates society. There is also a kind of power that does not come from virtue. But that kind of power ultimately acts to destroy the self, hurt other people, and poison society.

That sort of power is not the power of the truth. It is false, which is why we call it 'authoritarian power'. It is power that is not consequent upon virtue. True power must spring from virtue. Consequently, storing up virtue is storing up power.

An ordinary person experiences the lack of virtue as bad luck. Accumulating virtue brings good luck. The power that one generates by accumulating virtue produces good results in all that one does. This is what true luck is.

Because people who are not virtuous are powerless they can't really finish anything. They always seem to be in the wrong place at the wrong time. They blame their problems on misfortune and end up acquiescing to circumstance.

In a word, virtue augments luck. It improves one's good fortune.

Bad luck makes it impossible to do anything. And it leads to a lack of success in spiritual practice.

A *sakrdagamin* achieves perfect virtue, power, and wisdom. Nothing is impossible for him or her.

4. *Anagamin*——a saint who has leapt dimensions.

When a sage reaches this stage he enters the territory of sainthood.

He attains the wisdom of the higher dimensions, awakens spiritually, and becomes a saint who has the kind of power to interact with the spiritual world.

5. *Arhat*——a saint who transcends the dimensions.

This is a buddha who has reached nirvana.

The above is an attempt to explain the wisdom producing spiritual practices of the 7 systems and 37 elements of enlightenment. As these are rather abstract, I have tried to put them in a graphic form that may be easier to understand. (Please refer to illustration on page 137.)

Two distinctive practices included in Agon-shu's regimen of spiritual discipline are the practice of the fire ritual (*goma*) and the practice of waterfall asceticism.

Goma practice is a 'fire meditation' practice, or a *samadhi* of 'the realm of fire'.

Similarly, waterfall asceticism is a 'water meditation' practice, a kind of visualization of 'the essence of water'.

In my own personal experience of spiritual practice I found both of these *tapas*——the use of fire and water as a means of purifying and elevating mind and body——to be immensely effective, and so I have incorporated them into our overall regimen.

I believe that the performance of these two practices alone can bring anyone to the state of *sakrdagamin*.

Attaining nirvana is a very difficult thing to do. I do

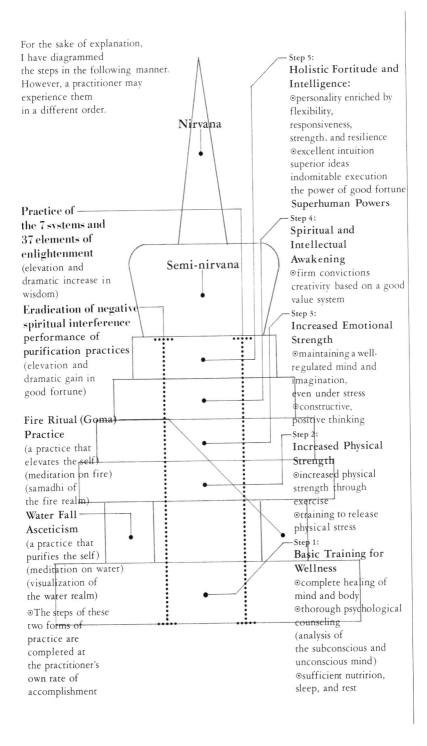

For the sake of explanation,
I have diagrammed
the steps in the following manner.
However, a practitioner may
experience them
in a different order.

Nirvana

Step 5:
**Holistic Fortitude and**
**Intelligence:**
⊙personality enriched by
flexibility,
responsiveness,
strength, and resilience
⊙excellent intuition
superior ideas
indomitable execution
the power of good fortune
**Superhuman Powers**

**Practice of**
**the 7 systems and**
**37 elements of**
**enlightenment**
(elevation and
dramatic increase in
wisdom)

Semi-nirvana

Step 4:
**Spiritual and**
**Intellectual**
**Awakening**
⊙firm convictions
creativity based on a good
value system

**Eradication of negative**
**spiritual interference**
performance of
purification practices
(elevation and
dramatic gain in
good fortune)

Step 3:
**Increased Emotional**
**Strength**
⊙maintaining a well-
regulated mind and
imagination,
even under stress
⊙constructive,
positive thinking

**Fire Ritual (Goma)**
**Practice**
(a practice that
elevates the self)
(meditation on fire)
(samadhi of
the fire realm)

Step 2:
**Increased Physical**
**Strength**
⊙increased physical
strength through
exercise
⊙training to release
physical stress

**Water Fall**
**Asceticism**
(a practice that
purifies the self)
(meditation on water)
(visualization of
the water realm)

⊙The steps of these
two forms of
practice are
completed at
the practitioner's
own rate of
accomplishment

Step 1:
**Basic Training for**
**Wellness**
⊙complete healing of
mind and body
⊙thorough psychological
counseling
(analysis of
the subconscious and
unconscious mind)
⊙sufficient nutrition,
sleep, and rest

not have the confidence that I can guide every practitioner to that point. However, I do believe that I can lead anyone to a state of semi-nirvana. Though, of course, the success of any practice ultimately depends on the efforts and enthusiasm of the practitioner.

# Afterword

I trust that you have found this comparison between the greatest intellectual achievement of the human race, the wisdom of philosophy, and the wisdom of the Buddha's nirvana, to be of interest.

The wisdom of academia, on the one hand, and the wisdom of religion, on the other. Are these completely different from one another or do they have something in common?

I began this investigation with the supposition that there must be some point within their highest reaches where these two forms of wisdom meet.

And, in fact, I found that there is. They do have a point of intersection.

I discovered this in the lineage of Greek philosophy that runs through Pythagoras, Socrates, and Plato.

This book summarizes what I found. I hope to pursue this topic more thoroughly in the future.

It may be difficult for the Westerner to understand the quintessence of Buddhism when it is explained only from the Buddhist perspective. I thought that including an explanation from the philosophical standpoint might make this understanding easier, and hope that this book has been helpful in that regard.

January 5, 2000
The author's birthday

**Addendum**
The record of a lecture delivered at
The National Buddhist Seminary
of China (Buddhist College)
(Dec. 13, 1999)

# About Agon-shu
# by
# Seiyu Kiriyama
The Chief Abbot of
the Agon Sect of Buddhism

Good day to members of the Seminary.

It has been a while since I have had the pleasure of being here with you. Almost a year has passed since my last visit. That day, Nov. 10, 1998, marks an occasion that I will remember for the rest of my life.

I received the great honor of being awarded an honorary degree of Professor Emeritus from this institution. To top it off, I received the honorary diploma from someone for whom I have the deepest respect, Dr. Zhao Puchu. Dr. Zhao is president of the Buddhist Association of China and the National Buddhist Seminary of China. He had written out the diploma in his own hand.

As you know, Dr. Zhao is considered the greatest calligrapher in China. His work is worth more than its weight in gold, because it is now almost impossible to come by. And he has reached a very venerable age. This famous calligrapher is the one who had personally inscribed the certificate that I was given.

This honorary diploma has become one of my family's most treasured heirlooms.

Subsequently, in August of this year, a delegation of 10 people from the seminary visited Agon-shu headquarters in Kyoto, Japan.

The head of the delegation was the Vice President of the Seminary Rev. Chuan Yin. He attended our ancestral prayer service on August 16th and gave a dharma talk to the congregation of more than 1000 people who were there. In his discourse, he said:

> Agon-shu, based as it is on the Agama Sutras, puts the fundamental tenets of Buddhism into practice: the Four Noble Truths, the Noble Eight-fold Path, and the Twelve-Linked Chain of Dependent Origination. These tenets are the core of the Buddha's teachings.
>
> We too believe that by actualizing these tenets we can purify people's minds and bring joy and happiness to their material and spiritual lives.

The audience was very impressed with the talk. After the service was over members of the congregation were overheard to say, "What an excellent sermon!" "I wish he had spoken longer." I hope Rev. Chuan Yin will visit us again and honor us with another dharma-talk. I have such a fond memory of that time.

Today I would like to tell you a bit about Agon-shu.

I established the Buddhist sect known as Agon-shu on April 8, 1978. So it has a history of only 21 years. You may laugh that I even use the word history, because it was formed such a short time ago.

However, I take great pride in the fact that it is the oldest Buddhist order in Japan, and like to claim that "Agon-shu is the newest and the oldest religious sect in the country."

I can say this because, as Rev. Chuan Yin noted, Agon-shu is based on the Agama Sutras.

As you know, the Agama Sutras, the oldest sutras that

exist, are the original sutras that Shakyamuni Buddha taught. So they are important not just because they are old, but because they are the only sutras we have that the Buddha himself preached. All other Buddhist sutras were written later by people who lived after the time of Shakyamuni Buddha.

Of course, a certain number of these later sutras got mixed up into the compendium that we call the Agama Sutras. But the fact still remains that no other collection of sutras exists which record the actual words spoken by the Buddha. This is something that has been verified academically.

The sutras that the Buddha actually taught are also know as 'the Sutras of the Golden Words', and there wasn't even one sect in Japan that was based on them. The emergence of Agon-shu 21 years ago was the first time in Japanese history that a sect was founded on the basis of the direct teachings of Shakyamuni Buddha.

Japanese Buddhism is Mahayana Buddhism, and, as such, has traditionally been founded on Mahayana scripture.

A scholarly and historical comparison of the Mahayana sutras and the Agama Sutras shows, naturally, that the Agamas are clearly older. That is why I say, half in jest, that "Agon-shu is the oldest and the newest."

I did not begin by establishing Agon-shu. Actually, I founded another sect before this one. The first sect was called Kannonjikeikai (The Kannon Benevolent Association). As the name implies, the sect was dedicated to the veneration of Kannon Bosatsu (Avalokiteshvara) as its principal deity and sought the blessings of Kannon's benevolence. Having this deity as its object of reverence placed the sect firmly within the lineage of Mahayana Buddhism.

I established the order in 1954. When I look back on it, it feels like I was really young at the time, only 32 years old. That was 46 years ago.

I led that organization for 24 years until I founded Agon-shu in 1978.

The Kannonjikeikai grew steadily. The congregation increased to 30,000 members, making it a mid-to-large-sized sect in Japan. If things had continued, I projected, along with other people, that the organization would become one of the major sects in the country. But then one day I suddenly abolished it and formed Agon-shu instead.

The people around me were shocked and mystified by my decision. People were very negative. One religion commentator offered this criticism: "The abrupt decision to change the principal deity and doctrines of a sect that has gotten so large is the act of a madman." An ecclesiastic wrote: "Has something happened to his mind, abandoning a growing sect, for, of all things, Hinayana Buddhism?"

Why did I turn away from Kannonjikeikai and towards Agon-shu?

Simply, it is because I had profound questions about the Buddhism that I had learned up to that point.

I believe that Buddhism can be broadly divided into two components:

Buddhist doctrine

and

Buddhist methodology

These two components, indeed, are those through which Buddhism comes into being.

Buddhist doctrine = teachings
In other words, dogma and ideology
Buddhist methodology = the power of the dharma
In other words, the power that results from the practice of the methodology

The Sanskrit word *dharma* can be translated as truth, actuality, essence. It was translated into Japanese and Chinese as the character *ho* (法), meaning law or method. But this is not what I mean when I use the word *ho*. I mean the power of the dharma, the inexpressible mystical power that comes from faith in Buddhism, the actualization of Buddhism, and the spiritual practices of Buddhism.

If Buddhism consisted only of dogma and doctrine it would amount to nothing more than a system of ethics and morality.

Buddhism becomes a religion through the fact that it has dharma (power). I am firmly convinced that this is true.

And so I turned from the study of Mahayana Buddhism to that of Shingon Buddhism, the esoteric sect that is grounded in the *Mahavairocana* and *Diamond Peak Sutras*. Shingon is a Mahayana sect, but it teaches the methodology of 'attaining Buddhahood in-this-very-body'.

Believing that this might be the true dharma that I was seeking, I became a practitioner of Shingon Buddhism and followed this path for about 10 years. I mastered the sect's highest esoteric techniques but in the end, again, plummeted into the depths of despair.

Because I concluded that the 'dharma' of Shingon Buddhism was nothing more than formulization. It had become mannered and formalistic.

This realization left me questioning my faith in Buddhism itself, and, at one point, I thought about leaving the tradition entirely. And then I started thinking: "I've read almost all of the major sutras of Mahayana Buddhism, but I've never read the Agama Sutras, which are relegated to the ranks of Hinayana, or 'lesser vehicle', sutras. It may be a waste of time, but I should at least take a look at them. If I find nothing there, I'll leave this tradition. It'll be goodbye Buddhism."

I got hold of a collection of the Chinese Canon of the Agama Sutras. The canon classifies the sutras according to four divisions: the *Dirgha-agama* (Long Discourses), the *Madhyama-agama* (Medium-length Discourses), the *Samyukta-agama* (Grouped Discourses) and the *Ekottara-agama* (Discourses Treating Enumerations). Altogether the collection consists of approximately 2080 fascicles. It took me a year and a half to read through them.

It was extremely difficult. I didn't have any teacher or elder to guide me. I did it completely by myself. I'd consult the Buddhist dictionary, but there was still a mountain of terms and phrases that I couldn't understand. There were some nights when I couldn't even understand one full line. I learned to just leave these alone and keep going and, as I did so, the meanings would mysteriously begin to become clear to me.

Before I finished my task I started to feel a great sense of elation. The method of spiritual practice I had been seeking these many long years was in there!

What I discovered was the wellspring, the point of origin, of the methods that Shingon taught as the way to 'attain Buddhahood in-this-very-body', the methods that had become so mannered and formalistic.

Thankfully, I discovered a jewel hidden deep within the Agama Canon: the 'method of spiritual practice for attaining Buddhahood' known as 'the 7 systems and 37 elements of enlightenment'.

Due to the constraints of time, I will just list the names of these 7 systems:

The Four Foundations of Mindfulness
The Four Right Kinds of Striving
The Four Bases of Spiritual Power
The Five Faculties
The Five Powers
The Seven Enlightenment Factors
The Noble Eightfold Path

These 7 systems are made up out of 37 elements, or curricula.

I now refer to this method as the '7 systems and 37 curricula that lead to the realization of sacred wisdom'. Each item involves specific techniques of meditation, contemplation, and sustained practice (*tapas*).

I found it very suprising that none of my predecessors in Japan had focused on these precious techniques before.

The reason for this oversight is probably because when the great Chinese religious genius T'ien-t'ai Master Chih-i devised his system of classification known as 'The Five Periods and the Eight Teachings' he placed the Agama

Sutras in the category of Hinayana scripture, and that is how they came to be known.

Why is the 7 system and 37 element method of spiritual practice so precious? Let me explain.

The ultimate aim of Buddhism is to attain nirvana. The Buddha states this time and again in his teachings, leaving no room for doubt.

If this is the case, then what do we have to do to get there? The whole thing boils down to this one basic point. This is what I was thinking about when I dug so extensively into the Buddhist sutras. This is what I was looking for when I read through the entire Chinese Canon.

And then, right before I was about to give up in despair, I discovered what I was seeking inside of the Agama Sutras.

When I think about it, one reaches the state of nirvana by attaining the highest supreme wisdom known to humankind.

This being true, then this system of spiritual practice must be one that cultivates and elevates wisdom.

The 7 systems and 37 elements come right to the point.

These are the practices that have the power to elevate a human being's level of wisdom.

And this is the reason I have dubbed them the '7 systems and 37 curricula that lead to the realization of sacred wisdom'.

One of the excellent attributes of this system is that it leads one to elevate one's wisdom in a graduated way.

In lay terminology, we could say that it engenders a

progression from

ordinary intelligence → brilliance → genius → great genius → super great genius.

Practicing this system of spiritual discipline may not lead everyone to the realization of nirvana, but I believe it will enable anyone to reach the prior levels of attainment.

The 21st century is the age of wisdom. Only the most advanced wisdom of the human race will be able to open up the future of the material world that is now heading towards a dead-end.

The science and technology that were supposed to bring us comfort and convenience instead threaten our very existence. Human wisdom is the only thing that can save us.

Now, indeed, is the time when we must cultivate wisdom.

I hope you see now why I liken the 7 systems and 37 elements to a precious jewel.

When all of this became clear to me, I decided that I would do whatever it took to get the information out into the world.

It made me wonder what to do.

I knew that if I founded a sect based on the Agama Sutras and called it Agon-shu it would antagonize the Japanese Buddhist establishment. I would be asking for a fight. They might even destroy me.

Why did I want to go ahead and willingly rock the boat when things with Kannonjikeikai were going along so smoothly? I couldn't decide what to do.

I couldn't make up my mind for 3 years. Maybe I was making a terrible mistake. Maybe I was just being dogmatic and biased. I kept vacillating back and forth.

But in the end I decided I had to take the chance. Shakyamuni Buddha spent his lifetime teaching this 'method for attaining Buddhahood'. And yet this teaching had been buried in obscurity because it was called Hinayana. Wasn't this like the Buddha himself was being obscured? And wasn't it my responsibility to reveal this to the world?

I was afraid that if I refused to act out of fear of failure, I would repent it at the time of my death. I would lament the fact that I hadn't founded Agon-shu when I had the chance. I would go to hell, because regret that you can't undo causes descent into the lower realms. In the end, I prepared myself to fail. I would establish the sect! I would have the courage of my convictions!

I went ahead and began Agon-shu.

Just as I thought, I was attacked on all sides by the Buddhist establishment.

But then most of the members of Kannonjikeikai, many of whom I expected to leave when I began Agon-shu, stayed with the new sect. This was an enormous source of strength for me. It helped me to withstand the slander, criticism, and abuse I received from the other Buddhist groups, and, in the end, I won.

Isn't the warm welcome that I have received from the Chinese Buddhist Association and the Buddhist Seminary the greatest proof of this victory?

In addition, I have received undreamed of honors from

Zhongshan University and Peking University as well. I have made such dear friends overseas that it moves me to tears. I offer you my deepest gratitude.

I'd like to add one final comment. I have never stopped venerating Kannon. My faith is as strong today as it was at the time of the Kannonjikeikai. No, I must say that it has gotten even stronger.

Thank you all so much for your time and kind attention.

## Sources:

Gallup, George, *The Miracle Ahead*, Harper & Row, New York, 1964.

*The Middle Length Discourses of the Buddha*, translated by Bhikkhu Nanamoli and Bhikkhu Bodhi, Wisdom Publications, Boston, 1995.

Plato, *The Last Days of Socrates*, translated by Hugh Tredennick and Harold Tarrant, Penguin Books, London, 1954.

*The Questions of King Milinda*, translated from the Pali by W. Rhys Davids, Dover Publications, Inc., New York, 1963.

Bhattacharyya, Benoytosh, *An Introduction to Buddhist Esoterism*, Oxford University Press, London, 1932.

## ABOUT THE AUTHOR

### Seiyu KIRIYAMA

Founder of Agon Shu Buddhist Association;
Professor Emeritus of Peking University;
Professor Emeritus of Zhongshan University;
Professor Emeritus of the National Buddhist Seminary of
China (Buddhist College);
Member of the Board of Directors, University of San Francisco;
Professor Emeritus and Honorary Doctor of Philosophy,
National University of Mongolia;
Honorary Doctor of Philosophy, Academy of Science Mongolia;
Honorable Doctorate Degree in Journalism and Mass Communication,
Thammasat University;
Honorary Fellow of School of Oriental and African Studies,
University of London;
Visiting Professor and Honorary Dean of the Nyingmapa
Tibetan Buddhist College;
Honorary Archbishop of the Siam Sect of Sri Lankan Buddhism;
Title of the Highest Rank of the Clergy of Myanmar Buddhism;
Director of the Chinese International Qigong Research Center (Beijing);
Honorary Member of the Dutch Treat Club, New York;
Honorary Ninth Rank, Japanese Go Association;
The Specially-invited Vice-President of Chinese Go Association.

### Author of 58 books,

including "Agon Buddhism as the Source of
'Shamatha (Tranquillity) and Vipashyanā (Insight)',"
"21st Century: The Age of *Sophia*,"
"You Have Been Here Before: Reincarnation,"
"The Wisdom of the *Goma* Fire Ceremony,"
"The Marvel of Spiritual Transformation,"
"Sacred Buddhist Fire Ceremony for World Peace 2001,"
and "The *Heart Sutra* Meditation,"
and the soon-to-be-released
"The Practitioner's Guide to Agon Buddhism."

## AGON SHU OFFICE ADDRESSES

**Main Temple**
Shakazan Daibodai-ji
Omine-cho, Yamashina-ku,
Kyoto City 607-8471,
JAPAN

**Kanto Main Office**
Agon Shu Kanto Betsuin
4-14-15 Mita, Minato-ku,
Tokyo 108-8318,
JAPAN
Tel. 81-3-3769-1931

**Kansai Main Office**
Agon Shu Kansai So-honbu
Jingumichi Agaru, Sanjodori,
Higashiyama-ku,
Kyoto City 605-0031,
JAPAN
Tel. 81-75-761-1141

**Hawaii Branch Office**
Agon Mission of Hawaii
The Tradewinds B-1-C,
1720 Ala Moana Blvd.,
Honolulu, Hawaii 96815,
U.S.A.
Tel. 1-808-949-4652

**Europe Branch Office**
Agon Shu UK
3 Queen Square, London WC1N 3AU,
England, UK
Tel. 44-20-7278-1988

**Brazil Branch Office**
Associacao Budista Agon Shu
Rua Dr. Nogueira Martins,
247 Saude,
CEP: 04143-020-Sao Paulo-SP,
BRASIL
Tel. 55-11-5581-9776

**Canada Branch office**
Agon Shu Canada Buddhist
Association
1255 Yonge St., Suite 302,
Toronto, Ontario M4T 1W6,
CANADA
Tel. 1-416-922-1272

**Taipei Main Office**
Agon Shu Taipei Honbu
1F.No.27-6, Sec.2, Chung-Cheng
East Rd., Tamshui, Taipei,
TAIWAN
Tel. 886-2-2808-4601

**Kaohsiung Branch Office**
Agon Shu Takao Shibu
No.975 Jung Hua 5th Rd.,
Chian Jen Sec., Kaohsiung,
TAIWAN
Tel. 886-7-537-2002

# 21st Century: The Age of *Sophia*

21世紀は智慧の時代【英語版】

2000年6月1日　第1版第1刷発行
2006年3月15日　第1版第7刷発行

著　者……桐山靖雄
　　　　　ⓒ 2000 by Seiyu Kiriyama
訳　者……ランディ・ブラウン
発行者……森真智子
発行所……株式会社平河出版社
　　　　　〒108-0073東京都港区三田3-4-8
　　　　　電話03(3454)4885　FAX03(5484)1660
　　　　　振替00110-4-117324
装　幀……谷村彰彦
印刷所……日本写真印刷株式会社
用紙店……中庄株式会社